quickfixes
{with mixes}

Fast Cooking with Bagged, Bottled & Frozen Ingredients

from the editors of
Southern Living

ISBN-13: 978-0-8487-3331-5
ISBN-10: 0-8487-3331-2
Library of Congress Control Number: 2009925689

Printed in the United States of America
First Printing 2010

Oxmoor House, Inc.
VP, Publishing Director: Jim Childs
Editorial Director: Susan Payne Dobbs
Brand Manager: Daniel Fagan
Senior Editor: Rebecca Brennan

Quick Fixes With Mixes
Editor: Susan Hernandez Ray
Project Editor: Vanessa Lynn Rusch
Senior Designer: Melissa Jones Clark
Director, Test Kitchen: Elizabeth Tyler Austin
Assistant Director, Test Kitchen: Julie Christopher
Test Kitchen Professionals: Allison Cox, Julie Fisher Gunter,
    Kathleen Royal Phillips, Catherine Crowell Steele,
    Ashley T. Strickland
Photography Director: Jim Bathie
Senior Photo Stylist: Kay E. Clarke
Associate Photo Stylist: Katherine Eckert Coyne
Production Managers: Terri Beste Farley, Tamara Nall

Contributors
Copy Editor: Rhonda Richards
Proofreader: Dolores Hydock
Food Stylists: Margaret Dickey, Alyson Haynes, Iris O'Brien
Indexer: Mary Ann Laurens
Interns: Chris Cosgrove, Georgia Dodge, Perri Hubbard,
    Allison Sperando, Christine Taylor

Southern Living®
Executive Editor: Scott Jones
Food Editor: Shannon Sliter Satterwhite
Senior Writer: Donna Florio
Senior Food Editors: Shirley Harrington, Mary Allen Perry
Senior Recipe Editor: Ashley Leath
Assistant Recipe Editor: Ashley Arthur
Test Kitchen Director: Lyda Jones Burnette
Assistant Test Kitchen Director: Rebecca Kracke Gordon
Test Kitchen Specialist/Food Styling: Marian Cooper Cairns,
    Vanessa McNeil Rocchio
Test Kitchen Professionals: Norman King, Pam Lolley, Angela Sellers
Senior Photographer: Ralph Anderson, Jennifer Davick
Photographer: Beth Dreling Hontzas
Senior Photo Stylist: Buffy Hargett

To order additional publications, call 1-800-765-6400
    or 1-800-491-0551

For more books to enrich your life, visit oxmoorhouse.com

To search, savor, and share thousands of recipes, visit myrecipes.com

{contents}

It's a fact:

Our lives are busier than ever. All the items that fill our daily schedules—from soccer practice to work deadlines to homework—cut into the time we have to plan and prepare supper. We also know that whether you're a beginner in the kitchen or a seasoned cook, now more than ever, **you need practical and delicious dinnertime solutions your family will enjoy.** That's why we're so excited about *Southern Living® Quick Fixes With Mixes.*

Our fast-paced lives have redefined the way we cook and have shaped our choice of recipes for our magazine. We've streamlined ingredient lists and methods as well as broadened our use of convenience products. This cookbook combines our years of expertise, kitchen-tested recipes, and best time-saving tips, all in an effort to create and showcase **real recipes for real people like you.**

One of the cookbook's most exciting features is the "Speed-Scratch Secret," which lets you in on some of our Test Kitchen's favorite hints and tips. Because **we understand just how busy you are**, we tell you, from chapters such as "Quick-Fix Appetizers" to "Main Dishes in Minutes," how much time you need to prepare each recipe and when a recipe can be made ahead. You'll find this to be an indispensable tool. What's more, we include more than 150 mouth-watering photographs (which also provide simple ideas for plating and garnishing for entertaining). I hope the more than 150 recipes and ideas in *Southern Living® Quick Fixes With Mixes* make each day a little bit easier for you.

Happy cooking!

Scott Jones
Executive Editor

be a speed-scratch cook

Preparing delicious meals for family and friends with minimal time and effort is a snap with a little preparation. ✸ Start by getting your kitchen organized and you'll quickly see how efficiency can save you time. ✸ **Next, get in the habit of making meal plans and shopping for convenience products.** ✸ And discover how easy it is to make batches of your own convenience products and make-ahead meals.

{ organize a time saving kitchen }

By stirring a few simple ingredients into bagged, boxed, or bottled items or using quick mixes and other convenience products, you can put homestyle recipes on your table without starting from scratch. And with these recipes there's never more than 15 minutes of hands-on prep time. Here's how.

✳ Store wooden spoons, rubber and metal spatulas, tongs, wire whisks, cooking spoons and forks, and kitchen shears in a jar near your cooktop and mixing center. Store pot holders close to the oven, cooktop, and microwave for quick access.

✳ Place bottles and boxes in your cupboard on a pullout tray where you can easily see the ingredients that you need.

✳ Stock your kitchen with must-have cooking gadgets and appliances to save time and energy. Purchase duplicates of things you use most often, such as measuring cups and spoons.

✳ Attach a magnetic shopping list to the refrigerator door for jotting down items to purchase as you think of them.

{ shop for convenience items }

Deli Items:

* diced tomatoes
* marinated beans
* prechopped onion
* sliced olives

Pantry Staples:

* bottled pasta sauce
* bouillon base
* canned beans
* canned tomatoes: diced, plain, seasoned
* canned whole-kernel corn
* chopped green chiles
* oils: olive, sesame, canola
* peppers in adobo sauce
* pesto sauce
* seasoning blends:
  * Cajun blend
  * Mediterranean blend
  * Mexican blend
  * Asian blend

{ make meal plans }

✳ Develop a repertoire of about 12 recipes your family loves. Bookmark them with sticky notes, or keep copies in a binder.

✳ Check your weekly calendar to determine just how many nights you'll be able to cook. Plan menus once a week for those nights.

✳ Do the bulk of your shopping once a week at a full-service supermarket; then plan one or two return trips to pick up perishables. Consider making those trips to mini-markets or to specialty grocers where access in and out is faster than larger grocery chains.

✳ Put your groceries through checkout in categories so they'll be bagged that way. When you arrive home, you'll be able to put away items quickly because they'll already be sorted.

Refrigerator and Freezer Items:

* bagged carrots
* bagged lettuce
* broccoli florets
* frozen fish
* frozen mixed vegetables
* jarred minced garlic

* mashed potatoes
* prechopped veggies
* precooked chicken: chopped, sliced, shredded
* prepared hummus
* preshredded cheese

{ make your own convenience items }

✳ Use preshredded cheese from the dairy aisle, or shred your own cheese and save a few pennies. You can even preshred a pound of cheese and freeze it in 1-cup portions to have on hand when for casseroles and toppings.

✳ Buy ground chuck when it's on sale; brown, drain, and freeze in 1-lb. portions.

✳ Roast a couple of whole chickens like the deli does; chop the meat, and freeze in 1-cup portions.

✳ Prechop onion, celery, and green pepper and refrigerate or freeze them in useful portions.

{ cook for now and later }

☀ Prepare a double batch of a casserole. Serve one now, and freeze another for later.

☀ Bake a double batch of muffins, waffles, or pancakes, and freeze the leftovers up to 1 month. Reheat in the toaster oven or microwave.

☀ Cook extra rice, and freeze in individual or family-size portions up to 1 month. Simply microwave to thaw.

☀ Freeze single-size portions of soup, casseroles, or other leftovers for lunch boxes or solo dinners.

Vegetable Soup Nov.

Mixed Vegetables Nov.

Vegetable Soup Nov.

quick-fix appetizers

Serving up tasty nibbles is a cinch with these recipes and handy helpers from the supermarket. ✺ Items such as prepackaged crostini, deli-cut vegetables, and preshredded cheeses help jump-start the preparation for party starters. ✺ **Many of these recipes can be prepared entirely or partially a day or two ahead of time.** ✺ Select serving containers ahead of time, too, so you'll be refreshed and ready to party!

Keep these three ingredients on hand to whip up a quick and tasty appetizer.

prep:
5
min.

Quick Fiesta Dip

prep: 5 min. • cook: 2 min. • other: 5 min.

makes 1½ cups

1 (9-oz.) package frozen corn niblets
1 (12-oz.) jar thick-and-chunky mild salsa
1 cup (4 oz.) shredded Colby or Cheddar cheese

1. Cook corn according to package directions; drain.

2. Pour salsa into a 9-inch glass pie plate; stir in corn. Cover with plastic wrap; fold back a small section of wrap to allow steam to escape. Microwave at HIGH 2 minutes or until bubbly.

3. Sprinkle cheese over salsa; cover with plastic wrap. Let stand 5 minutes or until cheese is melted. Serve with corn chips or tortillas.

start with...

✳ frozen corn
✳ bottled salsa
✳ preshredded cheese

speed-scratch SECRET

Frozen vegetables, such as the frozen corn used here, are great to keep on hand in order to enjoy out-of-season produce all year long. You may cook the corn called for here in boiling water on the stove-top or in the microwave.

kitchen secret:
grating cheese

Use preshredded cheese from the dairy aisle, or shred your own cheese and save a few pennies. You can even shred cheese ahead and freeze it in 1-cup portions to have on hand when you need it.

prep:
15
min.

start with...

* ✳ prechopped onion
* ✳ canned black beans
* ✳ bottled lime juice

Quickly snip fresh cilantro in a small cup using kitchen shears instead of dirtying the cutting board.

This tangy salsa is great served with chips as an appetizer, or spoon it over shredded lettuce as a salad.

Black Bean Salsa

prep: 15 min.
makes about 3 cups

1	plum tomato
1	avocado
⅓	cup chopped red onion
1	(15-oz.) can black beans, rinsed and drained
1½	Tbsp. chopped fresh cilantro
1	Tbsp. olive oil
2	Tbsp. lime juice
⅛	tsp. dried crushed red pepper
⅛	tsp. salt

1. Dice tomato. Peel, seed, and dice avocado. Combine tomato, avocado, onion, beans, and cilantro in a bowl.

2. Whisk together oil and next 3 ingredients. Toss with bean mixture. Cover and chill, if desired. Serve with corn chips or tortillas.

Warm salsa? You bet. It's just right for chilly weather.

prep:
15
min.

Bacon-and-Greens Salsa

prep: 15 min. • cook: 17 min.

makes 4 cups

8   bacon slices

1   (16-oz.) package frozen mixed greens, thawed and drained

½   medium-size sweet onion, chopped

1   tsp. jarred minced garlic

1½ cups frozen corn, thawed

1   serrano chile pepper, minced

¼   tsp. salt

¼   tsp. pepper

2   Tbsp. cider vinegar

1. Cook bacon in a large skillet over medium-high heat 7 to 9 minutes or until crisp; remove bacon, and drain on paper towels, reserving 2 Tbsp. drippings in skillet. Crumble bacon.

2. Sauté greens, onion, and garlic in hot drippings 7 to 10 minutes or until tender. Stir in corn and next 3 ingredients, and cook 3 minutes or until thoroughly heated. Remove from heat, and stir in vinegar. Sprinkle with bacon. Serve warm with pork rinds, sweet potato chips, and hot sauce.

start with...

✳ frozen mixed greens

✳ jarred minced garlic

✳ frozen corn

speed-scratch

We also loved this salsa over cream cheese (a great idea for leftovers). You can prepare the recipe up to a day ahead—just reheat the salsa before serving.

No one will guess this dish took just 10 minutes to make. It tastes like you chopped, peeled, and worked all day.

start with...

* bottled salsa
* bottled lime juice
* jarred minced garlic
* pita rounds
* olive oil cooking spray

speed-scratch
SECRET

Spraying pita rounds with olive oil cooking spray coats them much quicker than brushing them with butter or oil.

Dressed-up Salsa

prep: 10 min.

makes 2 cups

1   (24-oz.) jar chunky medium salsa
2½ Tbsp. lime juice
3   Tbsp. chopped fresh cilantro
1   tsp. jarred minced garlic
1   jalapeño pepper, seeded and chopped
Baked Pita Chips
Garnish: chopped fresh cilantro

1. Pulse first 5 ingredients in a food processor or blender 3 to 4 times or until mixture is thoroughly combined. Serve with Baked Pita Chips. Garnish with fresh cilantro.

baked pita chips

prep: 10 min. • cook: 12 min.

makes about 5 dozen

1   (8-oz.) package 4-inch pita rounds
Olive oil cooking spray
1½ tsp. coarsely ground kosher salt

1. Preheat oven to 350°. Separate each pita into 2 rounds. Cut each round into 4 wedges. Arrange in a single layer on ungreased baking sheets. Coat with olive oil cooking spray, and sprinkle evenly with 1½ tsp. kosher salt.

2. Bake at 350° for 12 to 15 minutes or until golden and crisp.

With plenty of veggies, sour cream, and cheese, this meatless appetizer is sure to please any crowd.

Layered Nacho Dip

prep: 5 min.

makes 8 cups

1	(16-oz.) can refried beans
2	tsp. taco seasoning mix
1	(6-oz.) container refrigerated avocado dip **or**
	1 cup guacamole
1	(8-oz.) container sour cream
1	(4.5-oz.) can chopped black olives, **drained**
2	large tomatoes, diced
1	small onion, diced
1	(4-oz.) can chopped green chiles
1½	cups (6 oz.) shredded Monterey Jack cheese

1. Stir together beans and seasoning mix; spread mixture into an 11- x 7-inch baking dish. Spread avocado dip and sour cream evenly over bean mixture. Sprinkle with olives and next 4 ingredients. Serve with corn chips or tortillas.

start with...

* ❋ canned refried beans
* ❋ taco seasoning mix
* ❋ refrigerated avocado dip
* ❋ canned chopped olives
* ❋ canned green chiles
* ❋ preshredded cheese

speed-scratch
SECRET

This dip can be made ahead and chilled up to 4 hours.

start with...

* deli-sliced cheese
* jarred minced garlic
* canned diced tomatoes and green chiles

Spicy White Cheese Dip

prep: 10 min. • cook: 3 hr.
makes about 8 cups

2   lb. white American deli cheese slices, torn
1   small onion, finely chopped
1   tsp. jarred minced garlic
2   (10-oz.) cans diced tomatoes and green chiles
¾   cup milk
½   tsp. ground cumin
½   tsp. coarsely ground pepper

1. Place all ingredients in a 6-qt. slow cooker. Cover and cook on LOW 3 hours, stirring gently every hour. Stir before serving. Change slow cooker to WARM. Serve with assorted chips.

speed-scratch
SECRET

To make ahead, spoon into quart-size freezer containers; freeze up to one month. Thaw overnight in the refrigerator. Microwave at HIGH, stirring every 60 seconds, until thoroughly heated.

kitchen secret:
chopping an onion

Trim the stem and root ends; discard. Remove the papery outer skins. Then stand the onion upright on a cutting board and cut a thin slice off one side. Make vertical slices through the onion to within ¼ inch of the bottom. Rotate the onion 90 degrees and repeat. Finally, turn the onion so that the cut side is flat on the board. Cut vertically through the onion.

Adobo sauce is a thick Mexican mixture made from chiles, vinegar, and spices that can be used as a marinade or as a sauce served on the side. Here, it packs a little punch into sour cream and prepared bean dip.

prep:
10
min.

Creamy Chipotle-Black Bean Dip

prep: 10 min.

makes 1 cup

½ cup sour cream

½ cup prepared black bean dip

1 tsp. minced chipotle peppers in adobo sauce

1 tsp. adobo sauce from can

¼ tsp. salt

Garnishes: chopped tomato, chopped avocado

1. Combine first 5 ingredients; stir well. Cover and chill up to 3 days. Garnish, if desired. Serve with tortilla chips.

kitchen secret:
pitting an avocado

Insert an 8- to10-inch chef's knife into the top where the stem was (it will be a darker area), and gently press down until you reach the pit. Strike the pit, and pierce it with the blade. Then twist and remove the knife; the pit will come with it.

start with...

✳ prepared black bean dip

✳ canned chipotle peppers

speed-scratch
SECRET

Chipotle peppers are smoked jalapeño peppers that are typically packed in an adobo sauce. Store any remaining adobo sauce in an airtight container in the refrigerator. Use it in teaspoonfuls as a quick way to jazz up soups and stews.

start with...

* refrigerated diced ham
* canned black-eyed peas

speed-scratch
SECRET

You can prepare dip 24 hours in advance, then reheat before serving

Serve this dip on New Year's Day to bring good luck for the year.

Black-eyed Pea-and-Ham Dip

prep: 15 min. • cook: 8 min.

makes 6 cups

½   cup diced country ham

2   (15.8-oz.) cans black-eyed peas, rinsed and drained

1   large tomato, finely chopped

2   green onions, sliced

1   celery rib, finely chopped

¼   cup chopped fresh parsley

2   Tbsp. olive oil

1   to 2 Tbsp. apple cider vinegar

1. Sauté ham in a lightly greased large nonstick skillet over medium-high heat 3 to 5 minutes or until lightly brown; stir in black-eyed peas and ¾ cup water. Reduce heat to medium, and simmer 8 minutes or until liquid is reduced by three-fourths. Partially mash beans with back of spoon to desired consistency.

2. Stir together tomato and next 5 ingredients. Spoon warm bean mixture into a serving dish, and top with tomato mixture. Serve with cornbread crackers.

prep:
10
min.

Ranch-Rémoulade Dip

prep: 10 min.

makes about 1½ cups

1	cup mayonnaise
¼	cup Ranch dressing
1	large dill pickle, diced (about ½ cup)
1	Tbsp. country-style Dijon mustard
1	Tbsp. dill pickle juice

1. Stir together all ingredients until blended. Cover and chill
until ready to serve. Serve with assorted precut fresh vegetables.
Store in refrigerator in an airtight container up to one week.

note: We tested with Grey Poupon Country Dijon Mustard.

start with...

* bottled Ranch
  dressing
* flavored mustard
* precut vegetables

kitchen secret:
julienne carrots

Julienning carrots into thin,
uniform matchsticks that are
2 to 3 inches long and ⅛ inch
wide make for great dippers.
Simply slice the four sides of a
cleaned, peeled carrot to form
rectangles. Cut the carrot into
⅛-inch strips. Stack the strips, and cut them into 2- to 3-inch-long
pieces.

speed-scratch
SECRET

Spoon this rich and creamy
rémoulade dip over sea-
food and poultry or use it
as a dressing over salads.

prep:
10
min.

start with...

* canned black-eyed peas
* bottled lemon juice
* jarred minced garlic

speed-scratch
SECRET

Hummus can be made up to two days in advance; just cover and chill.

You can find tahini (ground sesame seeds) near the peanut butter in most large supermarkets.

Black-eyed Pea Hummus

prep: 10 min. • other: 1 hr.
makes 2 cups

1	(15-oz.) can black-eyed peas, rinsed and drained
2	Tbsp. tahini
2	Tbsp. olive oil
¼	cup lemon juice
2	tsp. jarred minced garlic
½	tsp. salt
¼	tsp. ground cumin
½	tsp. freshly ground black pepper
⅛	tsp. ground red pepper

Olive oil
Garnish: fresh parsley

1. Process first 9 ingredients in a food processor until blended, stopping to scrape down sides. Gradually add 3 Tbsp. water until desired consistency. Cover and chill 1 hour. Drizzle with olive oil, and garnish, if desired. Serve with pita chips.

{ flavorful variation }

Traditional Hummus: Substitute 1 (15-oz.) can chickpeas, rinsed and drained, for black-eyed peas. Proceed with recipe as directed.

Warm Turnip Green Dip

prep: 15 min. · cook: 19 min.

makes 4 cups

5   bacon slices, chopped

⅔   cup chopped onion

2   garlic cloves, chopped

¼   cup dry white wine

1   (16-oz.) package frozen chopped turnip greens, thawed

12 oz. cream cheese, cut into pieces

1   (8-oz.) container sour cream

½   tsp. dried crushed red pepper

¼   tsp. salt

¾   cup freshly grated Parmesan cheese

1. Preheat oven to broil. Cook bacon in a Dutch oven over medium-high heat 5 to 6 minutes or until crisp; remove bacon, and drain on paper towels, reserving 1 Tbsp. drippings in Dutch oven.

2. Sauté onion and garlic in hot drippings 3 to 4 minutes. Add wine, and cook 1 to 2 minutes, stirring to loosen particles from bottom of Dutch oven. Stir in turnip greens, next 4 ingredients, and ½ cup Parmesan cheese. Cook, stirring often, 6 to 8 minutes or until cream cheese is melted and mixture is thoroughly heated. Transfer to a lightly greased 1½-qt. baking dish. Sprinkle evenly with remaining ¼ cup Parmesan cheese.

3. Broil 6 inches fom heat 4 to 5 minutes or until cheese is lightly browned. Sprinkle evenly with bacon. Serve with crackers.

start with...

✳ prechopped onion

✳ frozen turnip greens

✳ preshredded cheese

speed-scratch
SECRET

Transfer the dip to a 1- or 2-qt. slow cooker set on WARM so that guests can enjoy this creamy dip throughout your party. To make it spicier, serve your favorite brand of hot sauce on the side.

prep:
10
min.

start with...

* ✴ preshredded cheese
* ✴ bottled preserves
* ✴ packaged seasoned almonds

speed-scratch
SECRET

Make two batches of this quick recipe to serve a larger crowd. Serve the two side-by-side, offering a different flavor of preserves on each.

Almond-Cherry Cheese Spread

prep: 10 min.

makes 8 sevings

2   **Tbsp.** shredded Cheddar cheese
1   **(8-oz.) package cream cheese, softened**
¼   **cup** cherry preserves
2   **Tbsp. chopped** roasted salted almonds
1   **sliced green onion**

1. Sprinkle Cheddar cheese over softened cream cheese. Top with cherry preserves, salted almonds, and green onion. Serve with bagel chips, and, if desired, additional cherry preserves and chopped almonds.

kitchen secret:
slicing green onions

Diagonally sliced green onions make an eye-catching garnish. Slice diagonally by holding the knife at a 45-degree angle to the green onions and slicing to desired thickness.

This recipe stands out when paired with sun-dried tomato pita chips.

Southwest White Bean Spread

prep: 10 min.　•　other: 2 hr., 30 min.

makes about 1¼ cups

1 **tsp.** jarred minced garlic

1 **(15.5-oz.) can** cannellini **or** great Northern beans, **rinsed and drained**

⅓ **cup loosely packed fresh cilantro leaves**

3 **Tbsp.** lime juice

2 **Tbsp. olive oil**

½ **tsp. ground cumin**

1. Pulse garlic, next 5 ingredients, and 2 Tbsp. water in a food processor 3 or 4 times or until combined; process 1 to 2 minutes or until smooth, stopping to scrape down sides. Cover and chill at least 2 hours or up to 3 days. Let stand at room temperature 30 minutes before serving. Drizzle with additional olive oil, if desired. Serve with pita chips, sliced cucumbers, and olives.

{ flavorful variations }

Smoky Southwestern Spread: Prepare recipe as directed, adding 1½ Tbsp. chopped chipotle peppers in adobo sauce to mixture in food processor before pulsing. Chill as directed.

Green Chile Spread: Prepare recipe as directed, omitting water and adding 1 (4-oz.) can chopped green chiles to mixture in food processor before pulsing. Chill as directed.

start with...

✳ jarred minced garlic

✳ canned beans

✳ bottled lime juice

speed-scratch
SECRET

Southwest White Bean Spread—the perfect condiment for cold roast beef sandwiches—uses a can of great Northern beans for its extra-creamy texture. We also love it as a dip for seasoned baked pita chips, sliced cucumbers, and olives or as a tasty sauce drizzled over grilled chicken or pork.

start with...

* refrigerated bruschetta topping

* package of sun-dried tomatoes

* pretoasted baguette slices

speed–scratch
SECRET

Chopped fresh basil keeps this spread made from convenience products extra fresh-tasting.

This spread cozies up to pork, chicken, or grilled vegetables and makes a terrific dip for breadsticks.

Creamy Sun-dried Tomato Tapenade

prep: 10 min.

makes about 2 cups

1   (8-oz.) container refrigerated olive bruschetta topping, **drained**
1   (8-oz.) package cream cheese, **softened**
¼   cup extra-moist sun-dried tomato halves, **chopped**
1   Tbsp. chopped fresh basil

1. Stir together all ingredients with an electric mixer at medium speed until thoroughly combined. Cover and chill until ready to serve. Serve with toasted French baguette slices. Store in refrigerator in an airtight container up to one week.

note: We tested with Gia Russa Olive Bruschetta Topping and California Sun Dry Sun-Dried Tomato Halves.

Creamy Sun-dried Tomato Tapenade Crostini

prep: 10 min. • cook: 10 min.
makes 6 appetizer servings

1. Preheat oven to 350°. Thinly slice 1 (16-oz.) French bread baguette. Spread about 1 Tbsp. Creamy Sun-dried Tomato Tapenade on each baguette slice. Arrange on a baking sheet. Bake at 350° for 10 minutes.

Warmed Cranberry Brie

prep: 10 min. • cook: 5 min.
makes 8 appetizer servings

1   (13.2-oz.) Brie round
1   (16-oz.) can whole-berry cranberry sauce
¼   cup firmly packed brown sugar
2   Tbsp. spiced rum or orange juice
½   tsp. ground nutmeg
¼   cup prechopped pecans, **toasted**

1. Preheat oven to 500°.

2. Trim rind from top of Brie, leaving a ⅓-inch border on top. Place on a baking sheet.

3. Stir together cranberry sauce and next 3 ingredients; spread mixture evenly over top of Brie. Sprinkle with pecans.

4. Bake at 500° for 5 minutes. Serve with crackers or apple and pear slices.

start with...

* whole cheese round
* canned cranberry sauce
* packaged chopped pecans
* presliced fruit

speed-scratch SECRET

Serve this tasty appetizer with presliced apples and pears.

kitchen secret:
measuring brown sugar

Measure brown sugar by packing it firmly into a dry measuring cup; then level it off. Always use the measuring cup that holds the exact amount called for in a recipe.

start with...

❋ baking mix

❋ flavored feta cheese

speed-scratch
SECRET

Simple enough to put together on short notice, these quick-to-make crowd-pleasers can also be prepared up to a month ahead and frozen in an airtight container or zip-top plastic freezer bag. Reheat them straight from the freezer for 10 to 15 minutes, and then pass them around on a pretty tray.

Feta Cheese Squares

prep: 10 min. • cook: 30 min. • other: 10 min.
makes 5 dozen

2	cups all-purpose baking mix
1½	tsp. baking powder
¼	tsp. salt
1	cup milk
½	cup butter, melted
4	(4-oz.) packages feta cheese with garlic and herbs, crumbled
1	(8-oz.) container small-curd cottage cheese
3	large eggs, lightly beaten

Garnish: thyme sprig

1. Preheat oven to 350°. Stir together baking mix, baking powder, and salt in a large bowl. Stir in milk and next 4 ingredients, stirring just until dry ingredients are moistened. Spoon cheese mixture into a lightly greased 15- x 10-inch jelly-roll pan.

2. Bake at 350° for 30 minutes or until golden brown and set. Remove from oven, and let cool on a wire rack 10 minutes. Cut into 1½-inch squares, and serve immediately. Garnish with thyme sprig, if desired.

note: We tested with Bisquick All-Purpose Baking Mix.

Spinach-and-Parmesan Crostini

prep: 10 min. • cook: 10 min.

makes 1 dozen

1 (10-oz.) package frozen spinach, thawed

1 (8-oz.) package cream cheese, softened

1 cup freshly grated Parmesan cheese

¼ cup mayonnaise

1 tsp. jarred minced garlic

¼ tsp. freshly ground pepper

½ (16-oz.) French bread loaf, cut diagonally into ½-inch-thick slices

⅓ cup pine nuts

1. Preheat oven to 325°. Drain spinach well, pressing between paper towels to remove excess water.

2. Stir together spinach, cream cheese, Parmesan cheese, and next 3 ingredients in a medium bowl. Top each bread slice with 2 Tbsp. cheese mixture. Sprinkle with pine nuts. Place bread slices on a baking sheet.

3. Bake at 325° for 10 minutes or until thoroughly heated and nuts are toasted.

prep:
10
min.

start with...

* frozen spinach
* preshredded cheese
* jarred minced garlic

speed-scratch
SECRET

Prepare the spinach-and-cheese mixture up to a day ahead; cover and chill in an airtight container.

speed-scratch SECRET

To make ahead, simply fill the pastry with the spinach and cheese, and prepare the egg mixture. Cover both, and chill overnight. Next day, fill tarts with egg mixture, and bake.

Spinach-and-Gruyère Tarts

prep: 15 min. • cook: 30 min. • other: 5 min.

makes 16 tarts

2   (10-oz.) packages frozen tart shells

1   (10-oz.) package frozen chopped spinach, thawed and squeezed dry

1½ cups (6 oz.) shredded Gruyère cheese

4   large eggs

1½ cups half-and-half

½   tsp. salt

½   tsp. freshly ground pepper

Ground nutmeg

1. Preheat oven to 375°.

2. Arrange tart shells on a baking sheet. Fill each shell with about 1 Tbsp. each spinach and cheese.

3. Whisk together eggs and next 3 ingredients. Spoon egg mixture evenly into tart shells. Sprinkle lightly with nutmeg.

4. Bake at 375° for 30 to 35 minutes or until tarts are puffed and crust is lightly browned. Let stand 5 minutes before removing from foil pans.

note: We tested with Dutch Ann Frozen Tart Shells.

kitchen secret:
measuring liquids

Use a glass cup with a pouring spout to measure the half-and-half. Place it on a flat surface, and read at eye level, filling exactly to the line indicated.

Serve this savory pie as a starter for a ladies gathering, or enjoy it as a light supper with a tossed salad.

Tomato-Rosemary Tart

prep: 15 min. • cook: 24 min. • other: 20 min.

makes 4 servings

3	plum tomatoes
½	tsp. kosher salt
½	(17.3-oz.) package frozen puff pastry sheets, thawed
¼	cup (2 oz.) shredded mozzarella cheese
1	tsp. lemon zest
1	tsp. fresh rosemary
½	tsp. freshly ground pepper

1. Preheat oven to 400°. Cut tomatoes into ¼-inch slices, and place on a paper towel-lined wire rack. Sprinkle tomatoes with salt. Let stand 20 minutes. Pat dry with paper towels.

2. Unfold 1 puff pastry sheet on a lightly greased baking sheet. Arrange tomato slices in a single layer on pastry. Stir together cheese and next 3 ingredients in a small bowl. Sprinkle cheese mixture over tomatoes.

3. Bake tart at 400° for 24 to 27 minutes or until pastry is puffed and golden brown.

start with...

❋ **puff pastry sheets**

❋ **preshredded cheese**

speed-scratch
SECRET

Save time when peeling lots of tomatoes by giving them a quick dip in boiling water followed by a plunge in ice water. The process loosens their skins. Making a small x on the non-stem end will also help loosen the skins.

speed-scratch
SECRET

Because the flavor can be so intense, most recipes call for just a few capers to add sharpness. Remaining capers make a perfect garnish for meats, vegetables, and salads.

Tuna Niçoise Canapés

prep: 15 min.

makes about 3 dozen

2   (5.5-oz.) cans solid light tuna in olive oil, well-drained and flaked

¼   cup finely minced red onion

3   Tbsp. chopped kalamata or Niçoise olives

2   Tbsp. capers, drained

2   tsp. extra virgin olive oil

2   tsp. Dijon mustard

2   tsp. balsamic vinegar

¼   to ½ tsp. freshly ground pepper

⅛   tsp. kosher salt

Cucumber slices or endive leaves

1. Combine first 9 ingredients in a medium bowl. To serve, spoon tuna mixture onto cucumber slices or endive leaves.

note: We tested with Starkist Solid Light Tuna in Olive Oil.

Serve these meatballs from a slow cooker or chafing dish to keep them warm for a party, if you like.

prep:
5 min.

Spicy Party Meatballs

prep: 5 min. • cook: 45 min.

makes 8 dozen

1 (12-oz.) jar cocktail sauce
1 (10.5-oz.) jar jalapeño pepper jelly
½ **small sweet onion, minced**
½ (3-lb.) package frozen cooked meatballs

1. Cook first 3 ingredients in a Dutch oven over medium heat, stirring until jelly melts and mixture is smooth.

2. Stir in meatballs. Reduce heat, and simmer, stirring occasionally, 35 to 40 minutes or until thoroughly heated.

start with...

* bottled cocktail sauce
* bottled pepper jelly
* frozen meatballs

kitchen secret:
mincing an onion

To begin, see page 24 for instructions on how to chop an onion. Then use a chef's knife to run through the chopped onion in a rocking motion. Be sure to hold down the tip of the knife so that onion pieces don't go flying everywhere.

speed-scratch SECRET

We love the hint of spiciness the pepper jelly gives these glazed meatballs, but you may change it up if you'd like. Try grape jelly or jellied cranberry sauce.

prep:
10
min.

start with...

* precooked bacon
* presliced olives

speed-scratch
SECRET

Using precooked bacon saves time and makes cleanup a breeze.

Only four ingredients, but put together just so, they pack a wallop of first-course pleasure.

Bacon Appetizers

prep: 10 min. • cook: 7 min.
makes 2 dozen

1 lb. fully cooked bacon
1¾ cups (7 oz.) shredded Gouda cheese
1 cup mayonnaise
½ (16-oz.) package cocktail rye bread, lightly toasted
Garnishes: sun-dried tomato slivers, sliced ripe olives, fresh herbs

1. Preheat oven to 350°.

2. Crumble bacon. Combine bacon, cheese, and mayonnaise in a large bowl.

3. Spread mixture on rye bread slices. Place on ungreased baking sheets. Bake at 350° for 7 minutes or until cheese is bubbly. Garnish, if desired. Serve warm.

kitchen secret:
pitting an olive

To make easy work of pitting olives, you can use a pitter. If you don't have a pitter, place the olives on a cutting board. Place the flat side of a chef's knife on top, and press down using the heel of your hand. The olives will pop open, exposing the pits for easy removal.

Bacon Biscuit Cups

prep: 10 min. • cook: 22 min.

makes 10 biscuit cups

2 (3-oz.) packages cream cheese, softened

1 large egg

2 Tbsp. milk

½ cup (2 oz.) shredded Swiss cheese

1 green onion, chopped

1 (10-oz.) can refrigerated flaky biscuits

8 fully cooked bacon slices, chopped

Sliced green onions

start with...

✷ preshredded cheese

✷ can of biscuits

✷ precooked bacon

1. Preheat oven to 375°.

2. Place cream cheese and egg in a mixing bowl. Beat at medium speed with an electric mixer; add milk, beating until smooth. Stir in Swiss cheese and chopped green onion.

3. Separate biscuits into 10 portions. Pat each portion into a 5-inch circle, and press onto bottom and up sides of greased muffin cups, forming a ¼-inch edge. Sprinkle evenly with bacon; spoon cream cheese mixture into cups over bacon.

4. Bake at 375° for 22 minutes or until set. Sprinkle evenly with sliced green onions, lightly pressing into filling. Remove immediately from pan, and serve warm.

note: We tested with Pillsbury Refrigerated Flaky Biscuits and Oscar Mayer Ready to Serve Bacon.

speed-scratch

SECRET

For best results, be sure to keep the biscuits refrigerated until ready to use. Warm biscuit dough can be sticky and hard to handle.

prep:
12
min.

start with...

* packaged chopped nuts

* bottled balsamic glaze

speed–scratch
SECRET

This recipe is best assembled just before baking and served immediately after baking. Chop and mix ingredients ahead of time and assemble and bake at the last minute for a speedy appetizer that's ready in a snap.

Your favorite blue cheese is essential for decadence here. It is important to use a thick potato chip that will hold all of the heavy toppings in this recipe.

Blue Chip Nachos

prep: 12 min. • cook: 5 min.
makes 8 to 10 servings

1	(4-oz.) wedge Maytag or other blue cheese
3	Tbsp. tub-style cream cheese, softened
⅓	cup whipping cream
1	(5-oz.) bag lightly salted crinkle-cut potato chips
1	cup chopped walnuts, toasted
2	tsp. chopped fresh thyme
2	tsp. chopped fresh rosemary
2	to 3 Tbsp. bottled balsamic glaze

1. Preheat oven to 400°. Combine cheeses and whipping cream in a small bowl, stirring well. Spread whole potato chips in a double layer on a parchment paper-lined baking sheet. Dollop cheese onto potato chips. Sprinkle with walnuts.

2. Bake at 400° for 5 minutes or until heated. Remove from oven, and carefully slide chips and parchment paper onto a wooden board. Sprinkle with herbs; drizzle with desired amount of balsamic glaze. Serve immediately.

note: We tested with Kettle Potato Chips and Gia Russa Balsamic Glaze.

This quick, make-ahead recipe can be halved easily.

Balsamic Marinated Olives

prep: 9 min. • other: 8 hr., 30 min.

makes 9 cups

2   (6-oz.) cans ripe olives, **drained**

2   (6-oz.) jars pitted kalamata olives, **drained**

2   (7-oz.) jars pimiento-stuffed olives, **drained**

½   **cup olive oil**

½   **cup balsamic vinegar**

1   **Tbsp.** dried Italian seasoning

1. Place olives in a large nonmetallic bowl. Stir together oil, vinegar, and Italian seasoning. Pour over olives, stirring gently to coat. Cover and chill at least 8 hours.

2. Let stand at least 30 minutes at room temperature before serving.

start with...

✳ canned ripe olives

✳ jarred pitted olives

✳ jarred pimiento-stuffed olives

✳ dried Italian seasoning

speed-scratch
SECRET

Keep this easy appetizer up to one month in the fridge for a quick addition to salads or antipasto trays.

start with...

✳ seasoned breadcrumbs

✳ frozen steak fries

speed–scratch
SECRET

Serve these golden fries with a bottled marinara sauce for a quick dip.

If you like your fries with a little more zip, add 1 to 2 teaspoons of fajita seasoning.

Baked Potato Fries

prep: 8 min. • cook: 22 min.
makes 8 servings

1	**cup** Italian-seasoned breadcrumbs
1	**(28-oz.)** package frozen steak fries
3	**large eggs, lightly beaten**
3	**Tbsp. butter, melted**
1	**tsp. salt**

1. Preheat oven to 450°.

2. Place breadcrumbs in a zip-top plastic freezer bag. Dip fries in beaten egg; place fries in bag. Seal bag, and shake to coat. Place fries in a single layer on an ungreased 15- x 10-inch jelly-roll pan; drizzle with butter.

3. Bake, uncovered, at 450° for 22 minutes or until golden, turning once. Sprinkle with salt, and serve immediately.

kitchen secret:
baking with no mess

Line your baking sheet with parchment paper. Place ingredients on lined pan and bake as directed. Once done, remove parchment paper and toss.

A gourmet sea salt blend is the star ingredient that transforms plain almonds into a memorable snack.

Mediterranean Roasted Almonds

prep: 9 min. • cook: 45 min.

makes 5 cups

2 egg whites
2 tsp. Worcestershire sauce
2 (10-oz.) packages whole natural almonds
3 Tbsp. Mediterranean spiced sea salt
3 Tbsp. sugar
1 tsp. garlic powder
¼ tsp. dried crushed red pepper

1. Preheat oven to 300°.

2. Whisk together egg whites, Worcestershire sauce, and 1 Tbsp. water in a large bowl until frothy. Add nuts, stirring to coat.

3. Combine sea salt and next 3 ingredients in another bowl. Using a slotted spoon, transfer coated nuts to spice mixture; toss well to coat nuts. Transfer nuts with a slotted spoon to a lightly greased large rimmed baking sheet, spreading nuts into a single layer.

4. Bake at 300° for 45 minutes, stirring after 25 minutes. Remove almonds from oven; cool completely on wire racks to help nuts dry out and gain some crunch. Store in airtight containers up to 1 month.

note: We tested with McCormick Mediterranean Spiced Sea Salt.

start with...

✳ gourmet salt blend
✳ garlic powder
✳ crushed red pepper

speed-scratch
SECRET

There are a variety of seasoning blends on the market that speed up cooking with foreign flavors.

{ quick-fix appetizers }

Give it a Shot

Different-sized shot glasses arranged on a tiered serving stand quickly display snacks for guests. Combine a variety of size, shape, and color of different fruits, vegetables, and sweets.

Keep it Simple

An artful grouping of assorted cheeses with snappy accents is all that's needed to start a party. When selecting unfamiliar cheeses, make sure the flavors and textures partner well. Stronger-tasting cheeses are best served separately. Many stores offer samples and recommendations.

Take a Dip

Stir together ¾ cup sour cream and ¾ cup mayonnaise with 1 Tbsp. minced fresh parsley, 1 Tbsp. fresh chives, 1 tsp. fresh dill, 1 tsp. lemon zest, and 1 Tbsp. fresh lemon juice for a quick dip. Serve with assorted vegetables placed in glasses in sturdy recycled cup holders.

main dishes in minutes

Not much time to cook? No problem. Items such as prechopped produce, frozen vegetables, and bottled dressings help you prepare quick-and-easy delicious recipes. Fast recipes, quick ingredients, and make-ahead options help you get delicious dinners on the table in a hurry. Speed scratch secrets give you the inside scoop on getting meals together even faster.

Spinach-Ravioli Lasagna

prep: 10 min. • cook: 35 min.

makes 6 to 8 servings

1   (6-oz.) package fresh baby spinach, **thoroughly washed**

⅓   **cup refrigerated pesto sauce**

1   (15-oz.) jar Alfredo sauce

¼   **cup vegetable broth***

1   (25-oz.) package frozen cheese-filled ravioli (do not thaw)

1   cup (4 oz.) shredded Italian six-cheese blend

Garnishes: chopped fresh basil, paprika

1. Preheat oven to 375°. Chop spinach, and toss with pesto in a medium bowl.

2. Combine Alfredo sauce and vegetable broth. Spoon one-third of Alfredo sauce mixture (about ½ cup) into a lightly greased 2.2-qt. or 11- x 7-inch baking dish. Top with half of spinach mixture. Arrange half of ravioli in a single layer over spinach mixture. Repeat layers once. Top with remaining Alfredo sauce.

3. Bake at 375° for 30 minutes. Remove from oven, and sprinkle with shredded cheese. Bake 5 minutes or until hot and bubbly. Garnish, if desired.

*Chicken broth may be substituted.

note: We tested with Santa Barbara Original Basil Pesto and Bertolli Alfredo Sauce.

start with...

* **packaged prewashed spinach**
* **pesto sauce**
* **bottled Alfredo sauce**
* **frozen ravioli**
* **preshredded cheese**

speed-scratch
SECRET

While this dish calls for frozen ravioli, you can let it sit on the counter top for about 5 minutes before preparing the recipe to allow the frozen ravioli to separate easier.

start with...

* ready-to-serve Mexican rice

* canned beans

* canned green chiles

speed-scratch
SECRET

This recipe is perfect when you're cooking for two. But it can be doubled easily if you're cooking for a larger family.

Speedy Black Beans 'n' Mexican Rice

prep: 5 min. • cook: 3 min.

makes 2 servings

1 (8.8-oz.) **pouch** ready-to-serve Mexican Rice

1 (15-oz.) can black beans, **rinsed and drained**

1 (4.5-oz.) can chopped green chiles

2 **Tbsp. chopped fresh cilantro**

Toppings: sour cream, salsa, diced tomato, shredded Cheddar cheese

1. Cook rice according to package directions.

2. Combine black beans and green chiles in a microwave-safe bowl. Microwave at HIGH 90 seconds. Stir in rice and cilantro. Serve immediately with desired toppings.

{ flavorful variation }

Beefy Mexican Rice: Substitute a pound of cooked ground beef for the black beans and 1 cup salsa for the green chiles. Prepare as directed, omitting the toppings. Serve with corn chips or in lettuce leaves, if desired. Makes 4 servings.

kitchen secret:
chopping fresh cilantro

Wash the leaves in cold water, nip off the stems, and pat the leaves dry with paper towels. Hold the herbs tightly together on a cutting board with one hand; as you cut, move the fingertips of this hand to the blade. Use your other hand to hold the blade on the cutting board, rocking the knife up and down and scraping the cilantro into a pile as you cut.

Broiled Sirloin With Smoky Bacon Mushrooms

prep: 8 min. • cook: 22 min. • other: 5 min.

makes 4 to 6 servings

1	medium onion, cut vertically into thin slices
1	Tbsp. butter, melted
1	tsp. jarred minced garlic
2	(8-oz.) packages sliced fresh mushrooms
1¾	tsp. salt, divided
4	fully cooked hickory smoked bacon slices, crumbled
3	Tbsp. chopped fresh flat-leaf parsley
⅛	tsp. freshly ground pepper
2	(1-lb.) sirloin steaks (1¼ inches thick)
½	tsp. freshly ground pepper

1. Preheat broiler. Sauté onion in butter in a large skillet over medium heat 5 minutes until beginning to brown. Stir in garlic, mushrooms, and ¾ tsp. salt. Sauté 10 minutes or until mushrooms are tender and liquid evaporates. Stir in bacon, parsley, and ⅛ tsp. pepper.

2. While mushrooms cook, sprinkle both sides of steaks with remaining 1 tsp. salt and ½ tsp. pepper.

3. Broil 5½ inches from heat 7 minutes on each side or until desired degree of doneness. Let stand 5 minutes before slicing. Cut steaks into thin slices; arrange on a serving platter, and top with mushrooms.

prep:
8
min.

start with...

✳ jarred minced garlic

✳ presliced mushrooms

✳ precooked bacon

speed-scratch
SECRET

Serve this quick entrée with a simple side salad, or fold it into a flour tortilla to serve as a wrap.

start with...

✳ canned pineapple

✳ bottled salsa

✳ precooked rice

speed–scratch

SECRET

Grilling the pineapple slices and scallions alongside the meat preps them simultaneously for a quick stir into bottled salsa to serve on the side.

Grilled Steak With Pineapple Salsa

prep: 4 min. • cook: 6 min. • other: 5 min.

makes 4 servings

1   (8-oz.) can pineapple slices, **drained**
2   **Tbsp. brown sugar**
½   **tsp. kosher salt, divided**
1   **(1-lb.) flat-iron steak**
2   **scallions**
½   **cup** chunky salsa
Precooked rice

Garnish: grilled scallion

1. Spray cold grill rack with nonstick cooking spray. Preheat the grill to medium-high heat (350° to 400°).

2. Sprinkle pineapple with brown sugar and ¼ teaspoon salt. Sprinkle steak with remaining ¼ teaspoon salt. Grill steak, pineapple, and scallions, covered, 3 to 4 minutes on each side or until steak is desired degree of doneness and pineapple and scallions are tender.

3. Let steak stand 5 minutes; cut diagonally across grain into thin slices. Finely chop pineapple and scallions; place in a small bowl, and stir in salsa. Serve steak over rice and top with pineapple salsa. Garnish with grilled scallion, if desired.

kitchen secret:

trimming flat-iron steak

Flat-iron steak is flavorful, but the connective tissue that runs through the center can be tough. Slice away the connective tissue after cooking the steak.

Beef-and-Sausage Meatloaf With Chunky Red Sauce

prep: 15 min. • cook: 50 min. • other: 10 min.

makes 12 servings (2 meatloaves)

prep:
15
min.

- 1   lb. ground sirloin
- 1   lb. ground pork sausage
- 1   sleeve multigrain saltine crackers, **crushed**
- 1   (15-oz.) can tomato sauce
- 1   green bell pepper, diced
- ½   cup diced red onion
- 2   large eggs, lightly beaten

Chunky Red Sauce

1. Preheat oven to 425°. Line bottom and sides of 2 (8- x 4-inch) loaf pans with aluminum foil, allowing 2 to 3 inches to extend over sides; fold foil down around sides of pan. Lightly grease foil. Combine first 7 ingredients in a medium bowl. Shape mixture into 2 loaves. Place meatloaves in prepared pans.

2. Bake at 425° for 50 minutes or until a meat thermometer inserted into thickest portion registers 160°. Let stand 10 minutes. Remove meatloaves from pans, using foil sides as handles. Serve with Chunky Red Sauce.

chunky red sauce

prep: 5 min. • cook: 15 min.

makes about 3 cups

- 1   (26-oz.) jar vegetable spaghetti sauce
- 1   (14.5-oz.) can fire-roasted diced tomatoes
- 2   tsp. dried Italian seasoning
- ¼   tsp. pepper

1. Stir together all ingredients in a saucepan over medium heat. Cook, stirring frequently, 15 minutes or until heated.

start with...

✹ **sleeve of crackers**

✹ **prechopped onion**

✹ **bottled spaghetti sauce**

✹ **canned fire-roasted diced tomatoes**

speed-scratch SECRET

Cook once for two meals. Chill one meatloaf for at least 8 hours. Slice chilled meatloaf and reheat to create open-face sandwiches. You can substitute ground chuck or lean ground beef for the ground sirloin if that's what you have on hand.

start with...

✳ **canned tomatoes with herbs**

✳ **bottled marinara sauce**

✳ **seasoned breadcrumbs**

✳ **preshredded cheese**

speed-scratch
SECRET

To make ahead, prepare recipe as directed through Step 2. Shape into a 9- x 5-inch loaf, and cover with plastic wrap and aluminum foil. Freeze up to 2 months. Thaw in refrigerator 24 hours. Uncover and proceed with recipe as directed.

Tomato-Basil Meatloaf

prep: 10 min. • cook: 1 hr., 15 min. • other: 5 min.
makes 6 to 8 servings

1   lb. ground chuck

1   lb. lean ground pork

1   (14.5-oz.) can diced tomatoes with basil, oregano, and garlic, drained

⅓   cup marinara sauce

⅓   cup Italian-seasoned breadcrumbs

1   large egg, lightly beaten

1   tsp. salt

1   tsp. pepper

½   cup (2 oz.) shredded mozzarella cheese

1. Preheat oven to 375°. Stir together ground chuck and pork in a large bowl.

2. Process diced tomatoes in a blender or food processor 5 seconds or until slightly chunky, stopping to scrape down sides as needed. Stir tomatoes, marinara sauce, and next 4 ingredients into ground beef mixture just until combined.

3. Shape into a 9- x 5-inch loaf; place meatloaf on a wire rack in an aluminum foil-lined jelly-roll pan.

4. Bake at 375° for 1 hour. Top with mozzarella cheese, and bake 15 more minutes or until center is no longer pink. Let stand 5 minutes before serving.

Tostadas

prep: 5 min.   •   cook: 15 min.

makes 6 servings

1½ lb. lean ground beef

1   small onion, chopped

1   package taco seasoning mix

6   (8-inch) flour tortillas

1   (15-oz.) can kidney beans, rinsed and drained

1   large tomato, chopped

1   (8-oz.) bag preshredded iceberg lettuce

1   large avocado, peeled and chopped

2   cups (8 oz.) shredded sharp Cheddar cheese

Toppings: sour cream, salsa

1. Cook first 3 ingredients in a large skillet over medium heat, stirring until beef crumbles and is no longer pink; drain and set aside.

2. Pour oil to a depth of ¼ inch into a heavy skillet. Fry tortillas, 1 at a time, in hot oil over high heat 20 seconds on each side or until crisp and golden brown. Drain on paper towels.

3. Layer beef mixture, beans, tomato, and next 3 ingredients on warm tortillas. Serve with desired toppings.

prep:
5
min.

start with...

✸ taco seasoning mix

✸ canned beans

✸ preshredded lettuce

✸ preshredded cheese

✸ bottled salsa

speed-scratch
SECRET

Packaged taco seasoning flavors ground beef for Tex-Mex dishes quickly. It is now available in low-sodium varieties, if you prefer.

prep: 10 min.

start with...

* taco seasoning mix
* canned green chiles
* canned soup
* preshredded cheese
* bottled salsa

speed-scratch
SECRET

For easy removal and cleanup, line the baking dish with foil before spraying it with cooking spray.

Serve these tasty enchiladas over precooked Mexican rice.

Smothered Enchiladas

prep: 10 min. • cook: 25 min.
makes 8 servings

2⅓ lb. ground beef
1 (1.25-oz.) package mild taco seasoning mix
1 (4.5-oz.) can chopped green chiles, **divided**
2 (10¾-oz.) cans cream of chicken soup
1 (16-oz.) container sour cream
8 (8-inch) flour tortillas
2 cups (8 oz.) shredded Cheddar cheese
Garnishes: salsa, sour cream, green onion curls, chopped fresh cilantro

1. Preheat oven to 350°. Cook ground beef in a large skillet, stirring until it crumbles and is no longer pink; drain. Stir in taco seasoning mix and half of chopped green chiles; set aside.

2. Stir together remaining green chiles, soup, and sour cream. Pour half of soup mixture into a lightly greased 13- x 9-inch baking dish. Spoon beef mixture evenly down centers of tortillas; roll up. Place, seam sides down, over soup mixture in baking dish; top evenly with remaining soup mixture and cheese.

3. Bake at 350° for 25 minutes or until thoroughly heated. Garnish, if desired.

Tex-Mex Lasagna

prep: 7 min. • cook: 23 min.
makes 8 servings

1½ **lb. ground round**

1 **tsp.** jarred minced garlic

1 **(15-oz.)** can black beans, **rinsed and drained**

1 **(8-oz.)** package preshredded sharp Cheddar cheese, **divided**

2 **Tbsp. chili powder**

½ **tsp. ground cumin**

1 **(10-oz.)** can diced tomatoes with green chiles, **drained**

1 **(8-oz.) container sour cream**

1 **(16-oz.) bottle** chunky salsa

6 **(10-inch) flour tortillas**

1. Preheat oven to 425°. Cook beef and garlic in a large nonstick skillet over medium-high heat, stirring until beef crumbles and is no longer pink; drain.

2. Combine beef mixture, black beans, 1 cup cheese, and next 5 ingredients. Line a lightly greased 9- x 13-inch baking dish with 2 tortillas. Spoon one-third of beef mixture over tortillas. Repeat layers twice. Sprinkle with remaining cheese.

3. Bake at 425° for 15 minutes or until cheese melts.

prep:
7
min.

start with...

* jarred minced garlic
* canned beans
* preshredded cheese
* canned tomatoes with green chiles
* bottled salsa

speed-scratch SECRET

Both salsa and diced tomatoes with green chiles come in versions with varying heat levels for you to pick.

kitchen secret:
using fresh garlic

If you'd rather prep fresh garlic than use jarred, use a garlic press. Just place a peeled clove in the gadget, and press to force it through the tiny holes.

start with...

- ✳ package of shells and cheese
- ✳ canned beans
- ✳ canned tomatoes with green chiles

speed-scratch
SECRET

Browning the beef for this recipe while the pasta cooks helps you get dinner on the table in a hurry. Mixing the ingredients in the same skillet helps keep cleanup time to a minimum.

At the tasting table, this delicious recipe was our hands-down favorite over any boxed hamburger meal.

Chili-Cheeseburger Mac-and-Cheese

prep: 10 min. • cook: 15 min.
makes 4 servings

1   (12-oz.) box shells and cheese
1   lb. ground beef
1   tsp. chili powder
¼   tsp. ground cumin
1   (15-oz.) can kidney beans, rinsed and drained
1   (14.5-oz.) can diced tomatoes with mild green chiles
2   Tbsp. chopped fresh parsley

1. Prepare shells and cheese according to package directions.

2. Meanwhile, brown beef in a 12-inch (2½-inch-deep) non-stick skillet or Dutch oven over medium-high heat, stirring often, 8 minutes or until no longer pink; drain and rinse under hot running water. Return beef to skillet; stir in chili powder and cumin. Cook 2 minutes. Add beans, tomatoes, and ¼ cup water. Cook 5 to 8 minutes or until most of liquid has evaporated.

3. Stir prepared pasta into beef mixture, and sprinkle with chopped fresh parsley. Serve immediately.

note: We tested with Velveeta Shells & Cheese Original and Del Monte Diced Tomatoes with Zesty Mild Green Chilies.

Skillet Ziti

prep: 4 min. • **cook: 25 min.**
makes 8 servings

8   oz. uncooked ziti
1   lb. ground round
1   (10-oz.) package frozen chopped onion, **thawed and drained well**
½   tsp. salt
¼   tsp. freshly ground pepper
1   (26-oz.) jar tomato and basil pasta sauce
1   (8-oz.) container sour cream
⅓   cup shredded Parmesan cheese
1   (8-oz.) package shredded Italian six-cheese blend

1. Cook pasta according to package directions. Drain and set aside.

2. While pasta cooks, cook beef, onion, salt, and pepper in a large skillet over medium-high heat, stirring until beef crumbles and is no longer pink; drain.

3. Stir in pasta sauce; cook 1 minute or until thoroughly heated. Add pasta, stirring to coat.

4. Combine sour cream and Parmesan cheese. Stir into pasta mixture. Sprinkle Italian cheese blend over pasta mixture. Cover, reduce heat to medium, and cook 5 minutes or until cheese melts.

prep:
4
min.

start with...

✸ **frozen prechopped onion**
✸ **bottled pasta sauce**
✸ **preshredded cheese**

speed-scratch
SECRET

Skillet ziti cooks up twice as fast as the traditional oven-baked version—plus it's creamier and cheesier!

start with...

* bottled barbecue sauce
* can of cola

speed-scratch
SECRET

f you don't have a slow cooker, place roast in a lightly greased Dutch oven; stir together barbecue sauce and cola, and pour over roast. Before placing lid on top of Dutch oven, cover roast with a double layer of aluminum foil. Bake, tightly covered, at 325° for 3½ hours or until tender.

This super-simple recipe delivers big flavor. Reduce the fat but not the flavor in this juicy cut of pork by preparing it a day ahead. Cool the barbecue, and refrigerate overnight. Remove and discard any solid fat before reheating the pork.

Slow-cooker BBQ Pork

prep: 5 min. • cook: 6 hr.
makes 6 servings

1   (3- to 4-lb.) shoulder pork roast
1   (18-oz.) bottle barbecue sauce
1   (12-oz.) can cola soft drink

1. Place pork roast in a 6-qt. slow cooker; pour barbecue sauce and cola over roast.

2. Cover with lid, and cook on HIGH 6 to 7 hours or until meat is tender and shreds easily. Serve with slaw and steak fries.

note: We tested with Sticky Fingers Memphis Original Barbecue Sauce.

kitchen secret:
cleaning the slow cooker

Buy clear, heavy-duty plastic liners made to fit 3- to 6½-qt. oval and round slow cookers. Just fit the plastic liner inside your slow cooker before adding the recipe ingredients. When the cooker is empty, just toss the liner.

Bacon-Wrapped Pork Tenderloin

prep: 10 min. • cook: 23 min. • other: 10 min.
makes 4 servings

1 (¾- to 1-lb.) pork tenderloin
1 tsp. steak seasoning
3 bacon slices, cut in half crosswise
Hot cooked grits
Garnish: rosemary sprig

1. Preheat oven to 425°. Remove silver skin from pork tenderloin, leaving a thin layer of fat covering the pork. Sprinkle seasoning over pork. Wrap pork with bacon slices, and secure with wooden picks. Place pork on a lightly greased wire rack in an aluminum foil-lined roasting pan.

2. Bake at 425° for 20 minutes or until a meat thermometer inserted into thickest portion registers 155°. Increase oven temperature to broil. Broil 5 inches from heat 3 to 5 minutes or until bacon is crisp. Remove from oven; cover pork with foil, and let stand 10 minutes or until thermometer registers 160°. Serve pork over grits. Garnish, if desired.

note: We tested with McCormick Grill Mates Montreal Steak Seasoning.

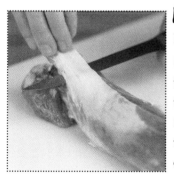

kitchen secret:
preparing pork tenderloin

Use a sharp boning knife to trim the tough silver skin from pork tenderloin before cooking. Leaving it on can cause the tenderloin to toughen and lose shape during cooking.

prep:
10 min.

start with...

* steak seasoning
* precooked or instant grits

speed-scratch SECRET

Pork tenderloin usually comes packed in pairs. Go ahead and season the other tenderloin in the package with your favorite spice blend. Wrap and freeze to jump-start another meal.

start with...

* boil-in-bag rice

* bottled barbecue
  sauce

* frozen prechopped
  onion

speed-scratch
SECRET

Using a slurry, which blends cornstarch or flour and water before adding it to a hot mixture, is a fast and easy way to thicken a sauce with no lumping.

Smothered Pork Chops Over Rice

prep: 5 min. • cook: 13 min.

makes 4 servings

2	extra-large bags boil-in-bag white rice
2	Tbsp. all-purpose flour
2	tsp. chili powder, divided
1	tsp. salt
⅛	tsp. pepper
4	(½-inch-thick) boneless pork loin chops
2	Tbsp. canola oil
½	cup bottled barbecue sauce
¼	cup frozen chopped onion
2	tsp. cornstarch

1. Prepare rice according to package directions; keep warm.

2. Meanwhile, combine flour, 1 tsp. chili powder, salt, and pepper in a shallow dish; dredge pork chops in flour mixture.

3. Heat oil in a large nonstick skillet over medium-high heat. Add chops, and cook 2 minutes on each side or until golden.

4. Combine barbecue sauce, onion, ¼ cup water, and remaining 1 teaspoon chili powder; pour over chops. Cover, reduce heat, and simmer 8 minutes or until chops are done. Remove chops from pan, and keep warm.

5. Combine cornstarch and 2 tsp. water, stirring until smooth. Add cornstarch mixture to sauce in pan; cook, stirring constantly, 1 minute. Divide rice evenly among plates; place chops over rice, and spoon sauce evenly over chops.

For an impressive presentation, perch these skillet chops on a mound of mashed sweet potatoes. Jazzing up a refrigerated fruit blend makes an oh-so-simple topping for the pork.

prep:
7
min.

Pork Chops With Shallot-Cranberry Sauce

prep: 7 min. • cook: 13 min.

makes 4 servings

4   boneless pork loin chops (¾ inch thick)

¾   tsp. salt, divided

½   tsp. freshly ground pepper

2   Tbsp. butter, divided

2   shallots, finely chopped (¼ cup)

1   (12-oz.) container cranberry-orange crushed fruit

1½   tsp. fresh thyme leaves

Frozen mashed sweet potatoes, cooked

1. Sprinkle both sides of pork with ½ tsp. salt and pepper. Melt 1 Tbsp. butter in a large skillet over medium-high heat. Add pork, and cook 4 to 5 minutes on each side or to desired degree of doneness. Remove pork from skillet; cover and keep warm.

2. Add remaining 1 Tbsp. butter to skillet, stirring just until butter melts. Add shallots, and sauté 1 to 2 minutes. Add crushed fruit and remaining ¼ tsp. salt to skillet; bring to a boil. Return pork and juices to skillet; cook 1 minute or until heated. Sprinkle with fresh thyme, and serve hot with warm mashed sweet potatoes.

start with...

❋ refrigerated cranberry-orange fruit blend

❋ frozen mashed sweet potatoes

speed-scratch
SECRET

Thyme is a quick herb to use because the leaves are so small that they often don't require chopping, especially when they're used as a garnish.

start with...

✳ bottled mango
chutney

speed-scratch
SECRET

Feel free to substitute chicken cutlets for chicken breasts—you'll save on prep time, because cutlets need no pounding or slicing before grilling.

Bottled chutney does double duty as a basting sauce and to serve on the side of these little chicken skewers. If you use wooden skewers, be sure to soak them for at least 30 minutes before threading the chicken. This prevents the skewer ends from burning.

Mango Chutney-Glazed Chicken Skewers

prep: 9 min. · cook: 6 min.

makes 4 or 5 servings

1½ tsp. chili powder

¾ tsp. salt

¼ tsp. ground cumin

4 (6-oz.) skinned and boned chicken breasts

2 tsp. vegetable oil

1 (9-oz.) bottle mango chutney (remove 3 Tbsp. chutney for brushing over chicken, reserving remaining portion for serving with grilled chicken)

1. Combine first 3 ingredients in a small bowl; set aside. Spray cold grill rack with nonstick cooking spray. Preheat grill to medium-high heat (350° to 400°).

2. Place chicken between 2 sheets of heavy-duty plastic wrap, and pound to ½-inch thickness, using a meat mallet or rolling pin. Cut each breast half lengthwise into 4 strips. Place chicken strips in a bowl; add chili powder mixture, and toss well to coat chicken. Drizzle chicken with oil.

3. Thread 1 chicken strip onto each of 16 (6-inch) skewers; brush chicken with 3 tablespoons chutney. Grill chicken, covered, 3 to 4 minutes on each side or until done. Serve with remaining chutney.

Chicken and Sausage Jambalaya

prep: 9 min. • cook: 21 min.
makes 6 servings

prep:
9
min.

1   lb. skinned and boned chicken breasts, cut into 1-inch pieces
2   tsp. Cajun seasoning, **divided**
2   tsp. canola oil
1   lb. smoked sausage, sliced
1   (10-oz.) package frozen seasoning blend, **thawed and drained**
2   tsp. jarred minced garlic
1   (14½-oz.) can diced tomatoes with zesty mild green chiles,
    undrained
1   extra-large bag boil-in-bag white rice, **removed from bag**
1½ cups chicken broth
Garnish: minced flat-leaf parsley

1. Combine chicken and 1 tsp. Cajun seasoning in a bowl.

2. Heat oil in a Dutch oven over medium-high heat. Add sausage and chicken; sauté 6 minutes or until browned on all sides. Remove from pan; drain.

3. Add seasoning blend and garlic to pan; sauté 2 minutes or until heated thoroughly. Add sausage, chicken, remaining 1 tsp. Cajun seasoning, tomatoes, rice, and broth to pan. Bring to a boil; cover and boil 11 minutes or until liquid is absorbed, stirring halfway through cooking time. Garnish, if desired.

start with...

* Cajun seasoning
* frozen seasoning blend
* jarred minced garlic
* canned tomatoes with green chiles
* boil-in-bag rice

speed-scratch
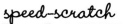
SECRET

Boil-in-bag rice speeds up the cooking time of this Creole favorite. But instead of cooking the rice separately in its bag, we add it straight to the pan so that it can absorb the liquid and all the savory flavors as it cooks.

start with...

✳ canned soup

SECRET

This recipe is a snap to lighten. Prepare the recipe as directed, using light butter; nonfat buttermilk; and reduced-sodium, reduced-fat cream of mushroom soup.

Tangy buttermilk turns a can of mushroom soup into a tasty sauce for chicken. Serve the entrée with steamed asparagus.

Buttermilk Baked Chicken

prep: 15 min. · cook: 35 min.

makes 4 servings

¼ cup butter

4 bone-in chicken breasts, skinned

½ tsp. salt

½ tsp. pepper

1½ cups buttermilk, divided

¾ cup all-purpose flour

1 (10¾-oz.) can cream of mushroom soup, undiluted

Paprika

Garnish: lemon wedges

1. Preheat oven to 425°. Melt butter in a lightly greased 13- x 9-inch baking dish in a 425° oven.

2. Sprinkle chicken with salt and pepper. Dip chicken in ½ cup buttermilk, and dredge in flour. Arrange chicken, breast sides down, in baking dish.

3. Bake at 425° for 15 minutes. Turn chicken, and bake 10 more minutes. Stir together remaining 1 cup buttermilk and cream of mushroom soup; pour over chicken, sprinkle with paprika, and bake 10 more minutes, shielding chicken with aluminum foil to prevent excessive browning, if necessary. Garnish, if desired.

Find the best quality pimiento cheese in the deli section of your supermarket, where it's available by weight or in prepackaged tubs. It has more Cheddar cheese and less processed cheese than many lower-priced varieties.

prep:
15
min.

Pimiento Cheese Chicken With Hot Buttered Grits

prep: 15 min. • cook: 10 min.

makes 4 servings

4   (6-oz.) skinned and boned chicken breasts

½   tsp. seasoned salt

¼   tsp. pepper

¾   cup premium-quality pimiento cheese

4   cups chicken broth

1⅓   cups uncooked quick-cooking grits

2   Tbsp. butter

1. Preheat broiler. Place chicken between 2 sheets of heavy-duty plastic wrap, and flatten to ¼-inch thickness, using a meat mallet or rolling pin. Sprinkle chicken with salt and pepper; place chicken on a lightly greased rack in a broiler pan.

2. Broil chicken 5 inches away from heat 5 minutes. Turn chicken, and spoon 3 Tbsp. pimiento cheese over each chicken breast, spreading to edges. Broil 5 more minutes or until cheese is bubbly and lightly browned.

3. Bring chicken broth to a boil in a large saucepan over medium-high heat. Reduce heat to low; whisk in grits. Cover and cook 5 to 7 minutes or until thickened, stirring occasionally. Remove from heat, and stir in butter. Serve with chicken.

start with...

* deli-style pimiento cheese
* quick-cooking grits

speed-scratch **SECRET**

To get dinner on the table faster, prepare the grits while the chicken is broiling.

prep:
10
min.

start with...

✳ seasoned salt

✳ canned soup

✳ Italian dressing mix

✳ presliced mushrooms

✳ frozen biscuits

speed-scratch
SECRET

I f you don't serve all the chicken at once, shred the leftover cooked chicken, and toss with hot cooked pasta. Or create a casserole or jump-start a filling for easy enchiladas or a fast pot pie.

Creamy Slow-cooker Chicken

prep: 10 min. • cook: 4 hr., 15 min.

makes 6 servings

6   skinned and boned chicken breasts (about 2½ lb.)
2   tsp. seasoned salt
2   Tbsp. canola oil
1   (10¾-oz.) can reduced-fat cream of mushroom soup
1   (8-oz.) package ⅓-less-fat cream cheese
½   cup dry white wine
1   (0.7-oz.) envelope Italian dressing mix
1   (8-oz.) package sliced fresh mushrooms
6   frozen extra-large sandwich-style biscuits

1. Sprinkle chicken with seasoned salt. Cook chicken, in batches, in hot oil in a large skillet over medium-high heat 2 to 3 minutes on each side or just until browned. Transfer chicken to a 5-qt. slow cooker, reserving drippings in skillet.

2. Add soup, cream cheese, white wine, and Italian dressing mix to hot drippings in skillet. Cook over medium heat, stirring constantly, 2 to 3 minutes or until cheese is melted and mixture is smooth.

3. Sprinkle mushrooms over chicken in slow cooker. Spoon soup mixture over mushrooms. Cover and cook on LOW 4 hours. Stir well before serving.

4. Prepare biscuits according to package directions. Serve chicken mixture over biscuits.

note: We tested with Good Seasons Italian All Natural Salad Dressing and Recipe Mix.

Chicken Thighs With Chunky Tomato Sauce

prep: 10 min. • cook: 23 min.
makes 4 to 6 servings

1	(22-oz.) package frozen mashed potatoes
2	lb. skinned and boned chicken thighs
1	Tbsp. Greek seasoning
2	Tbsp. olive oil
2	medium zucchini, chopped
½	cup diced onion
1	(14.5-oz.) can fire-roasted tomatoes with garlic, **undrained**
2	Tbsp. cold butter, cut up
1	Tbsp. red wine vinegar
¼	tsp. salt
¼	tsp. pepper

start with...

❋ frozen mashed potatoes

❋ Greek seasoning

❋ prechopped onion

❋ seasoned canned tomatoes

1. Prepare mashed potatoes according to package directions. Keep warm.

2. Meanwhile, sprinkle chicken with Greek seasoning. Cook chicken in hot oil in a large skillet over medium-high heat 7 to 8 minutes on each side or until done. Remove from skillet, and keep warm.

3. Reduce heat to medium. Add zucchini and onion to skillet, and sauté 2 to 3 minutes or until tender. Add tomatoes, and cook, stirring often, 7 to 10 minutes or until slightly thickened. Remove from heat, and stir in butter and next 3 ingredients.

4. Serve chicken over potatoes. Spoon sauce over chicken and potatoes. Serve immediately.

note: We tested with Ore-Ida Mashed Potatoes, Cavender's All Purpose Greek Seasoning, and Hunt's Fire Roasted Tomatoes Diced With Garlic.

speed-scratch **SECRET**

A splash of red wine vinegar and a can of fire-roasted tomatoes with garlic make this a stand-out that's ready in less than an hour. Serve with slices of fresh bread from the bakery.

start with...

* presliced mushrooms
* jarred minced garlic
* canned soup
* rotisserie chicken

speed-scratch
SECRET

We added a little white wine to this recipe to dress it up. If you don't have any on hand or prefer not to use wine, increase the milk to 1⅓ cups.

Snappy Smothered Chicken

prep: 10 min. • cook: 25 min.
makes 4 servings

1 (8-oz.) package wide egg noodles

1 tsp. paprika

1 tsp. dried thyme leaves, crumbled

½ tsp. salt

¼ tsp. pepper

3 Tbsp. butter

1 large onion, chopped

1 (16-oz.) package sliced mushrooms

2 tsp. jarred minced garlic

1 (10¾-oz.) can cream of mushroom soup

1 cup milk

⅓ cup dry white wine (optional)

1 rotisserie chicken, cut into serving pieces

2 Tbsp. chopped fresh parsley

1. Prepare noodles according to package directions. Keep warm.

2. Meanwhile, stir together paprika, dried thyme, salt, and pepper in a small bowl.

3. Melt butter in a large skillet over medium-high heat; add onion and mushrooms, and sauté 8 to 10 minutes or until onion is tender. Stir in garlic and paprika mixture; sauté 2 minutes. Add soup, milk, and, if desired, wine, and bring to a boil, stirring frequently. Add chicken pieces; spoon sauce over top of chicken. Reduce heat to low, and cook, covered, 10 to 15 minutes or until chicken is thoroughly heated. Stir in 1 Tbsp. parsley. Serve over hot cooked noodles. Sprinkle with remaining parsley.

Sprinkling sun-dried tomatoes and sliced fresh basil over the finished dish adds distinctive flavor and a pretty appearance.

prep:
10
min.

Sun-dried Tomato Chicken

prep: 10 min. · cook: 1 hr.

makes 6 servings

1   (4-lb.) package chicken pieces (3 breasts, 4 thighs, 3 legs)
1   cup sun-dried tomato vinaigrette with roasted red pepper dressing
½   tsp. coarsely ground pepper
Toppings: chopped sun-dried tomatoes, sliced fresh basil

1. Preheat oven to 400°. Arrange chicken pieces in a single layer in a lightly greased 13- x 9-inch baking dish. Pour dressing evenly over chicken pieces, and sprinkle with ground pepper.

2. Bake, uncovered, at 400° for 1 hour or until done, basting every 15 minutes. Sprinkle baked chicken with desired toppings.

note: We tested with Good Seasons Sun Dried Tomato Vinaigrette With Roasted Red Pepper Dressing.

kitchen secret:
softening sun-dried tomatoes

Here's the trick to softening the texture of sun-dried tomatoes: Buy them packed in oil, and then drain and rinse in hot water to remove oil. Chop tomatoes with a knife, or snip them into smaller pieces with kitchen shears.

start with...

✳ bottled dressing
✳ packaged sun-dried tomatoes

speed-scratch
SECRET

S ubstitute 6 skinned and boned chicken breasts for chicken pieces. Prepare recipe as directed, decreasing bake time to 30 minutes.

start with...

* prechopped onion
* jarred minced garlic
* bottled dressing

speed-scratch
SECRET

Use a food processor to dice the onion if you would rather use it than prechopped.

Skinned and boned chicken thighs contain a little more fat than breast meat, but they're very nutritious and hold moisture well.

Sweet-and-Sour Chicken and Rice

prep: 15 min. • cook: 1 hr.
makes 8 servings

½   tsp. salt

½   tsp. pepper

2   lb. skinned and boned chicken thighs

1   cup chopped onion

1   medium red bell pepper, cut into 1-inch strips

2   tsp. jarred minced garlic

1   cup uncooked long-grain rice

1   cup sweet-and-sour dressing

1   cup low-sodium, fat-free chicken broth

2   green onions, sliced

1. Sprinkle salt and pepper evenly over chicken thighs. Brown chicken in a Dutch oven coated with cooking spray over medium-high heat 2 to 3 minutes on each side or until browned. Remove chicken from pan, and set aside.

2. Add onion, bell pepper, and garlic to Dutch oven coated with cooking spray; sauté 5 minutes. Add rice; sauté 2 minutes or until rice is opaque.

3. Stir in dressing and broth. Add chicken pieces; bring to a boil. Cover, reduce heat, and simmer 45 minutes or until liquid is absorbed and chicken is done. Sprinkle with green onions.

note: We tested with Old Dutch Sweet & Sour Dressing.

Many of the ingredients for this hearty Mexican-style casserole can be kept in your pantry.

Santa Fe Chicken and Dressing

prep: 15 min. • cook: 40 min.

makes 4 to 6 servings

4	cups cubed country-style stuffing
2	cups chopped precooked chicken
1	(15½-oz.) can golden hominy, **drained**
1	(4.5-oz.) can chopped green chiles, **drained**
½	cup chopped red bell pepper
½	cup minced fresh cilantro
1	(10¾-oz.) can cream of mushroom soup, **undiluted**
1	(8¾-oz.) can cream-style corn
1	cup sour cream
2	tsp. ground cumin
1	cup (4 oz.) shredded Monterey Jack cheese

Tortilla chips (optional)

Salsa (optional)

1. Preheat oven to 350°. Combine first 6 ingredients in a large bowl; add soup and next 3 ingredients, stirring well. Spread in a lightly greased 2-qt. shallow baking dish.

2. Bake, covered, at 350° for 35 minutes or until thoroughly heated. Uncover and sprinkle with cheese; bake 5 more minutes or until cheese melts. Serve with tortilla chips and salsa, if desired.

start with...

* package of stuffing
* precooked chicken
* canned hominy
* canned green chiles
* canned soup
* canned corn
* preshredded cheese

speed-scratch
SECRET

Make the most of your chicken. Depending on the size, 1 chicken will yield 3 to 4 cups of chopped cooked meat. Remove the meat from the bones when it's still warm, and freeze up to one month in a zip-top plastic freezer bag.

prep: 13 min.

start with...

* frozen seasoning blend
* precooked chicken
* canned soup
* canned tomatoes with green chiles
* preshredded cheese

speed-scratch **SECRET**

Freeze casserole up to one month, if desired. Thaw in refrigerator overnight, and bake as directed.

Rediscovering the King Ranch Casserole brings back fond childhood memories. We've published several versions of this family favorite, and this one's the quickest yet. No sautéing is needed; just stir together the ingredients, and pop it in the oven.

King Ranch Chicken Casserole

prep: 13 min. • cook: 32 min.
makes 6 servings

1   **(10-oz.)** package frozen seasoning blend
2   **cups chopped** precooked chicken
1   **(10¾-oz.)** can cream of chicken soup
1   **(10¾-oz.)** can cream of mushroom soup
1   **(10-oz.)** can diced tomatoes and green chiles
1   **tsp. chili powder**
½   **tsp. garlic salt**
12   **(6-inch) corn tortillas**
2   **cups (8 oz.)** shredded Cheddar cheese, **divided**

1. Preheat oven to 350°. Stir together first 7 ingredients.

2. Tear tortillas into 1-inch pieces; layer one-third of tortilla pieces in a lightly greased 13- x 9-inch baking dish. Top with one-third of chicken mixture and ⅔ cup of cheese. Repeat layers twice.

3. Bake at 350° for 32 minutes or until casserole is thoroughly heated and bubbly.

Leftover turkey or a rotisserie chicken works equally well in this casserole. Crisp sourdough croutons are its crowning glory. Use bagged broccoli florets from the grocery produce section.

Chicken-and-Broccoli Cobbler

prep: 15 min. • cook: 30 min.

makes 4 servings

¼ cup butter, melted

3 cups cubed sourdough bread (6½ oz.)

½ cup preshredded Parmesan cheese

3 cups small broccoli florets

3 cups chopped cooked chicken

½ cup drained chopped roasted red bell pepper

1 (10-oz.) container refrigerated Alfredo sauce

½ cup sour cream

2 Tbsp. dry sherry

1. Preheat oven to 400°. Drizzle butter over bread cubes in a large bowl; sprinkle with cheese, and toss well.

2. Combine broccoli and next 5 ingredients in a large bowl. Spoon filling into a lightly greased 2-qt. rectangular or oval baking dish or individual baking dishes; top with bread cubes.

3. Bake, uncovered, at 400° for 30 minutes (20 to 25 minutes for individual cobblers) or until bubbly and top is toasted.

start with...

❋ preshredded cheese

❋ packaged broccoli florets

❋ precooked chicken

❋ jarred roasted bell pepper

❋ bottled Alfredo sauce

speed-scratch
SECRET

There's no need to pre-cook the broccoli—it will be crisp-tender when the casserole is bubbly.

prep:
10
min.

start with...

* precooked barbecue pork
* frozen corn
* package of pre-washed and torn lettuce
* preshredded cheese
* bottled barbecue sauce

speed-scratch SECRET

Instead of making your own barbecue dressing, purchase a bottle of barbecue sauce when you pick up your barbecue for the salad and use it by itself.

Warm Barbecue Salad

prep: 10 min. • cook: 35 min.

makes 6 servings

3   cups shredded barbecued pork
Barbecue Dressing, divided
1   cup frozen whole kernel corn, **thawed**
2   bacon slices, cooked and crumbled
1   (8-oz.) bag mixed salad greens
4   plum tomatoes, chopped
⅓   large red onion, sliced
⅔   cup shredded mozzarella cheese

1. Preheat oven to 350°. Stir together pork and 1 cup Barbecue Dressing in a lightly greased 9-inch square pan.

2. Bake, covered, at 350° for 35 minutes or until warm.

3. Toss together corn and next 4 ingredients. Top with warm barbecue mixture, and sprinkle with cheese. Serve immediately with remaining dressing.

barbecue dressing

prep: 10 min. • cook: 20 min.

makes 3 cups

1   (18-oz.) bottle barbecue sauce
⅓   cup firmly packed light brown sugar
½   cup honey
⅓   cup ketchup
1   Tbsp. butter
1   Tbsp. Worcestershire sauce
½   tsp. seasoned salt
1   tsp. lemon pepper

1. Stir together all ingredients in a saucepan; bring to a boil. Reduce heat; simmer, stirring occasionally, 10 minutes.

Chicken 'n' Spinach Pasta Bake

prep: 15 min. • cook: 1 hr.

makes 4 to 6 servings

8   oz. uncooked rigatoni

1   Tbsp. olive oil

1   cup finely chopped onion

1   (10-oz.) package frozen chopped spinach, **thawed**

3   cups cubed cooked chicken

1   (14.5-oz.) can Italian-style diced tomatoes

1   (8-oz.) container chive-and-onion cream cheese

½   tsp. salt

½   tsp. pepper

1½ cups (6 oz.) shredded mozzarella cheese

1. Preheat oven to 375°. Prepare rigatoni according to package directions.

2. Meanwhile, spread oil on bottom of an 11- x 7-inch baking dish; add onion in a single layer.

3. Bake at 375° for 15 minutes or just until tender. Transfer onion to a large bowl, and set aside.

4. Drain chopped spinach well, pressing between layers of paper towels.

5. Stir rigatoni, spinach, chicken, and next 4 ingredients into onion in bowl. Spoon mixture into baking dish, and sprinkle evenly with shredded mozzarella cheese.

6. Bake, covered, at 375° for 30 minutes; uncover and bake 15 more minutes or until bubbly.

{ flavorful variation }

Sausage 'n' Spinach Pasta Bake: Substitute 3 cups cooked, crumbled hot Italian sausage for 3 cups cubed cooked chicken. Reduce salt to ¼ tsp., and omit ½ tsp. pepper. Proceed with recipe as directed.

prep:
15 min.

start with...

✳ frozen spinach

✳ precooked chicken

✳ canned Italian-style diced tomatoes

✳ seasoned cream cheese blend

✳ preshredded cheese

speed-scratch SECRET

Keep pasta fresh longer and handy for quick meals by storing it in airtight containers.

prep:
15
min.

start with...

* canned stewed tomatoes

* canned tomato paste

* precooked chicken

speed-scratch SECRET

When cooking spaghetti, it's not necessary to first break the pasta into pieces. Simply hold one end of the pasta by the handful, and dip the other end into boiling water, pushing pasta gently until it softens enough to submerge.

Chicken Spaghetti

prep: 15 min. • cook: 20 min.
makes 6 to 8 servings

1   (12-oz.) package spaghetti
1   medium onion, chopped
1   small green bell pepper, chopped
1   (14-oz.) can chicken broth
1   (14¼-oz.) can Italian-style stewed tomatoes
1   (6-oz.) can Italian-style tomato paste
1   (16-oz.) package pasteurized processed cheese product, cubed
3   cups chopped precooked chicken

1. Prepare spaghetti according to package directions. Drain and keep warm.

2. Meanwhile, sauté onion and bell pepper in a Dutch oven coated with cooking spray over medium-high heat 3 to 4 minutes. Stir in broth, tomatoes, and tomato paste.

3. Bring to a boil; reduce heat, and simmer 10 minutes. Stir in cheese; cook 1 minute or until melted. Stir in pasta and chicken; cook 2 to 3 minutes or until thoroughly heated.

Cheesy Chicken Casserole

prep: 15 min. • cook: 30 min. • other: 5 min.

makes 4 to 6 servings

1   rotisserie chicken

1   (10¾-oz.) can chicken and mushroom soup

1   (8-oz.) container sour cream

¼   tsp. pepper

1   (8-oz.) package shredded sharp Cheddar cheese, **divided**

25 round buttery crackers, **coarsely crushed**

1. Preheat oven to 350°. Remove chicken from bones; discard bones and skin. Shred chicken. Stir together chicken, soup, sour cream, pepper, and 1½ cups cheese; spoon mixture into a lightly greased 2-qt. baking dish.

2. Combine remaining ½ cup cheese and cracker crumbs; sprinkle evenly over top.

3. Bake casserole at 350° for 30 minutes or until bubbly. Let stand 5 minutes before serving.

prep:
15
min.

start with...

* rotisserie chicken
* canned soup
* preshredded cheese
* sleeve of crackers

speed-scratch
SECRET

To quickly crush the crackers, place them in a zip-top plastic freezer bag, seal all but a small corner to allow air to escape, and crush with a rolling pin.

Any firm white fish fillets, such as orange roughy, grouper, or red snapper, will work well in this dish.

start with...

* frozen fish
* canned tomatoes with herbs
* deli olives
* jarred minced garlic
* precooked rice

speed-scratch
SECRET

Purchase just the amount of pitted olives you need at an olive bar or salad bar of large supermarkets instead of using canned and having leftovers to store.

Mediterranean Fish Fillets Over Rice

prep: 5 min. • cook: 15 min.
makes 4 servings

4   (6-oz.) frozen firm white fish fillets, **thawed**
¾   tsp. salt
½   tsp. pepper
1½ Tbsp. olive oil
1   (14½-oz.) can diced tomatoes with basil, garlic, and oregano, undrained
½   cup pitted kalamata olives, **halved**
2   Tbsp. lemon juice
1   tsp. jarred minced garlic
Warm cooked rice

1. Pat fish fillets dry with paper towels; sprinkle with salt and pepper. Heat oil in a large nonstick skillet over medium-high heat. Add fish; cook 3 to 4 minutes on each side or until browned.

2. Add tomatoes and next 3 ingredients to skillet. Cover, reduce heat, and simmer 9 to 10 minutes or until fish flakes easily with a fork. Serve fish and tomato mixture over warm rice.

Seared Halibut With Herbed Tomato Sauce

prep: 10 min. • cook: 18 min.

makes 4 servings

4   (6-oz.) frozen halibut fillets (½ inch thick), thawed

½   tsp. salt, divided

¼   tsp. pepper

2   tsp. extra virgin olive oil

½   medium onion, chopped

½   tsp. jarred minced garlic

1   Tbsp. drained capers

1   (14.5-oz.) can petite diced tomatoes with basil, garlic, and oregano

1. Pat fish dry with paper towels. Season fish with ¼ tsp. salt and ¼ tsp. pepper. Cook fish in hot oil in a large skillet over medium-high heat 3 to 4 minutes on each side or until fish flakes with a fork and is opaque throughout. Transfer fish to a serving platter, and keep warm.

2. Add onion and garlic to skillet, and sauté 1 to 2 minutes or until onion is tender. Stir in capers, and remaining ¼ tsp. salt; cook 1 minute. Reduce heat to low, add tomatoes, and cook, stirring occasionally, 10 minutes. Top fish with tomato mixture.

speed-scratch SECRET

If you don't have any halibut on-hand, the tomato mixture also tastes great served over chicken.

start with...

※ Italian dressing mix

※ peeled and deveined shrimp

※ packaged refrigerated fettuccine

speed-scratch SECRET

Put the pasta on to cook as you start the shrimp to have dinner on the table in record time.

138 main dishes in minutes

Sautéed Shrimp

prep: 10 min. • cook: 10 min.
makes 4 servings

¼   cup butter
1   (0.7-oz.) envelope Italian dressing mix
1   lb. peeled and deveined medium-size raw shrimp
1   (9-oz.) package refrigerated fettuccine

1. Melt butter in a large skillet over medium heat; stir in dressing mix. Add shrimp; cook, stirring constantly, 3 to 5 minutes or until shrimp turn pink. Cook pasta according to package directions. Serve shrimp immediately over pasta.

kitchen secret:
peeling and deveining shrimp

It's fastest to purchase shrimp that has already been peeled and deveined. But, if you'd like to start with shrimp in the shell, begin by peeling the shrimp. Then cut a shallow slit along the back of the shrimp using a sharp paring knife. Lift and remove the dark vein with the knife tip. Rinse shrimp under cold water; drain. One pound of shrimp in the shell equals ¾ pound of peeled and deveined shrimp.

Here's the perfect party recipe—
guests peel their own shrimp and
save you the work! Serve with French
bread to sop up the savory sauce.

prep:
10
min.

Garlicky Baked Shrimp

prep: 10 min. • cook: 25 min.

makes 6 servings

start with...

✴ bottled Italian
dressing

✴ jarred minced garlic

3 lb. unpeeled, large raw shrimp

1 (16-oz.) bottle Italian dressing

1½ Tbsp. freshly ground pepper

2 tsp. jarred minced garlic

2 lemons, halved

¼ cup chopped fresh parsley

½ cup butter, cut up

1. Preheat oven to 375°.

2. Place first 4 ingredients in a 13- x 9-inch baking dish, tossing to coat. Squeeze juice from lemons over shrimp mixture, and stir. Add lemon halves to pan. Sprinkle shrimp with parsley; dot with butter.

3. Bake at 375° for 25 minutes, stirring after 15 minutes. Serve in pan.

speed-scratch SECRET

To bake this when you're on vacation at the beach, purchase a large disposable roasting pan for easy cleanup.

start with...

* quick-cooking rice
* jarred minced garlic
* peeled and deveined shrimp
* frozen mixed vegetables

speed-scratch
SECRET

Use leftover rice, or make rice ahead and refrigerate, to help get supper on the table in a hurry. Starting with cooked and chilled rice not only saves time, but the end product is better.

The secrets of making good fried rice are high heat and minimal oil.

Shrimp Fried Rice

prep: 5 min. • cook: 16 min.

makes 4 servings

2	(3.5-oz.) bags quick-cooking long-grain rice
3	Tbsp. canola oil, divided
2	large eggs, lightly beaten
1	tsp. jarred minced garlic
¼	tsp. crushed red pepper
1	lb. peeled and deveined frozen raw shrimp, thawed
1½	cups frozen mixed vegetables, thawed
3	Tbsp. soy sauce

1. Cook rice according to package directions; set aside.

2. Meanwhile, place 1 Tbsp. oil in a large skillet over medium-high heat. Add eggs; cook 1 to 2 minutes, stirring frequently until scrambled. Remove from skillet, and set aside.

3. Heat remaining 2 Tbsp. oil in skillet; add garlic, crushed red pepper, and shrimp. Cook 2 minutes or until shrimp turn pink. Add vegetables, and cook until thoroughly heated. Stir in soy sauce, reserved rice, and scrambled eggs; cook 1 minute or until thoroughly heated.

{ quick-fix main dishes }

Fresh Fish in a Flash

Sprinkle fillets with seasoning blend and sauté 3 or 4 minutes, turning once. To check for doneness, gently lift the fish with a knife. Fully cooked fillets will begin to flake, changing from translucent to opaque.

Barbecue Sundae

Set up a station for guests or family to make their own sundaes. Simply spoon barbecue pork evenly into 12-oz. glasses. Top each with shredded cheese. Add store-bought deli slaw and chopped fresh cilantro. Dollop each serving with sour cream. Serve sundaes with tortilla wedges, lime wedges, fresh cilantro sprig, and prechopped pickle slices.

Taco Night

Set up a taco bar with toppings such as carrots, avocado, mango, onions, queso fresco, red cabbage, jalapeños, and salsa.

speedy soups & sandwiches

If you're looking for a simple supper, it doesn't get much easier than soup and sandwich night. ✹ Throw one or the other (or both!) together quickly when you get home, or pick one of the many make-ahead recipes to whip up a quick lunch-on-the-go the night before. ✹ Frozen and canned veggies make soup preparation simple and deli-sliced meats and cheeses keep sandwich-making a snap. ✹ A hearty soup or sandwich can be the ultimate one-dish meal.

Pick your favorite brand of barbecue sauce to guide the flavor from mild to spicy to smoky in this easy stew.

Easy Brunswick Stew

prep: 15 min. • cook: 50 min.

makes 12 servings

3 **pounds** shredded cooked pork

4 **cups** frozen cubed hash brown potatoes

3 **(14½-oz.)** cans diced tomatoes with garlic and onion

1 **(14½-oz.)** can whole kernel corn, **drained**

1 **(14½-oz.)** can cream-style corn

½ **cup** barbecue sauce

1 **Tbsp.** hot sauce

1½ **tsp.** salt

1 **tsp.** pepper

2 **cups** frozen lima beans **(optional)**

1. Stir together shredded pork, 4 cups water, next 8 ingredients, and, if desired, lima beans in a 6-qt. stockpot.

2. Bring mixture to a boil; cover, reduce heat, and simmer, stirring often, 45 minutes.

start with...

✹ precooked shredded pork

✹ frozen potatoes

✹ canned tomatoes with garlic and onion

✹ canned corn

✹ bottled barbecue sauce

✹ frozen lima beans

speed-scratch
SECRET

Pick up precooked and shredded pork at a barbecue restaurant, or look for refrigerated barbecue at the supermarket to jump-start this stew.

start with...

* prechopped onion
* jarred minced garlic
* canned chili hot beans

speed-scratch SECRET

Start with ground round; after browning the meat, there's virtually no fat to drain. The little bit of drippings there will add flavor.

Easy Texas Chili

prep: 2 min. • cook: 20 min.

makes 4 servings

1 **lb. ground round**
1 **cup** chopped onion
1 **tsp.** jarred minced garlic
1 **(16-oz.)** can chili hot beans, **drained**
1 **(6-oz.) can tomato paste**
1 **Tbsp. chili powder**

1. Combine first 3 ingredients in a Dutch oven; cook until beef is browned, stirring until it crumbles. Add beans, tomato paste, 1½ cups water, and chili powder; cover, reduce heat, and simmer 15 minutes, stirring occasionally.

kitchen secret: browning ground round

Don't add meat to a cold pan. Heat the pan until it's hot before adding the meat. And don't overcrowd your pan.

Canned tomatoes, canned beans, and a chili seasoning mix turn ground turkey and ground turkey sausage into a robust meal. Top the chili with sour cream and Cheddar cheese for extra flavor.

Turkey Chili

prep: 15 min. • cook: 50 min.
makes 6 servings

1   onion, chopped
1   green bell pepper, chopped
1   lb. ground turkey
1   lb. ground turkey sausage
1   tsp. vegetable oil
1   (16-oz.) can chili beans
2   cups tomato sauce
2   cups tomato juice
1   garlic clove, minced
1   (1.75-oz.) envelope chili seasoning mix
1   (10-oz.) can diced tomatoes and green chiles
1   tsp. sugar

Garnishes: sour cream, shredded Cheddar cheese

1. Cook onion, bell pepper, ground turkey, and sausage in hot oil in a Dutch oven over medium heat, stirring until meat crumbles and is no longer pink. Drain well.

2. Add chili beans and next 6 ingredients to Dutch oven; bring to a boil, stirring frequently. Reduce heat, and simmer 30 minutes, stirring occasionally. Garnish each serving, if desired.

start with...

✳ **canned chili beans**
✳ **canned tomato sauce**
✳ **canned tomato juice**
✳ **chili seasoning mix**
✳ **canned tomatoes with green chiles**

speed-scratch
SECRET

This chili makes a big batch and freezes well, so package any leftovers in single-serving containers for quick meals another day.

prep:

15

min.

start with...

❋ frozen fish

❋ frozen hash browns

❋ canned soup

❋ bacon bits

❋ jarred pimientos

speed-scratch
SECRET

Fish is hard to thaw evenly, but these fillets will thaw in about 15 minutes in a sink of cold water.

Frozen tilapia fillets are great to keep on hand for weeknight dinners.

So-Quick Seafood Chowder

prep: 15 min. • cook: 15 min.

makes 6 servings

12 oz. fresh or frozen orange roughy fillets, **thawed**

½ **(24-oz.)** package frozen hash browns with onions and peppers

1 **(12-oz.) can evaporated milk**

1 **(10¾-oz.)** can cream of potato soup, **undiluted**

¼ **cup** bacon bits

2 **tsp. chopped fresh dill or ¾ teaspoon dried dillweed**

¼ **tsp. salt**

¼ **tsp. pepper**

1 **(2-oz.)** jar diced pimientos, **drained**

1. Cut fish fillets into 1-inch pieces.

2. Bring hash browns to a boil in 1 cup water in a large saucepan; reduce heat to low, cover, and simmer 5 minutes or until tender.

3. Stir in evaporated milk and next 5 ingredients; return to a boil. Add fish and pimiento; cover, reduce heat, and simmer 3 to 5 minutes or until fish flakes easily. Serve immediately.

note: We tested with Ore-Ida Potatoes O'Brien and Hormel Real Bacon Bits.

prep:
15
min.

Potato-Vegetable Chowder

prep: 15 min. • cook: 15 min.

makes 6 servings

2   Tbsp. vegetable oil
1   **cup** chopped onion
3   Tbsp. all-purpose flour
2   cups milk
1   (10¾-oz.) can chicken broth
1   (10-oz.) package frozen chopped broccoli, **thawed**
½   (32-oz.) package frozen Southern-style hash browns **(4 cups)**
1   (8¼-oz.) can sliced carrots, **rinsed and drained**
1   cup (4 oz.) shredded sharp Cheddar cheese
¾   tsp. salt
½   tsp. pepper

1. Heat oil in a Dutch oven over medium-high heat. Add onion, and sauté until tender. Add flour, and cook, whisking constantly, 1 minute. Whisk in 1 cup milk and chicken broth until blended. Stir in remaining 1 cup milk, broccoli, hash browns, and carrots; cook over medium heat 7 minutes.

2. Stir in 1 cup cheese, salt, and pepper; cook 5 minutes.

start with...

* prechopped onion
* frozen broccoli
* frozen hash browns
* canned carrots
* preshredded cheese

speed-scratch
SECRET

Fresh ingredients combined with convenience products make for a winning recipe. Sprinkle some extra cheese on top of each serving for an added punch of flavor.

prep:
5
min.

start with...

✳ canned beans

✳ prechopped onion

✳ preshredded carrot

✳ canned ham

speed-scratch
SECRET

Preshredded carrot, found in the produce section or the deli, speeds up this simple soup and is handy to keep around for sprinkling into green salads.

Ham gives this soup a punch of flavor. Using canned ham keeps things simple.

White Bean Soup

prep: 5 min. · cook: 15 min.
makes 3 servings

1	**(16-oz.)** can navy beans, **undrained**
1	**(15.8-oz.)** can great Northern beans, **undrained**
¼	**cup** chopped onion
½	**cup** preshredded carrot
¼	**cup butter, melted**
1	**(5-oz.)** can chunk ham, **drained and flaked**

1. Combine beans in a large saucepan; mash slightly with a potato masher. Stir in 1 cup water, and cook over low heat until thoroughly heated.

2. Meanwhile, sauté onion and carrot in butter over medium-high heat until onion is tender. Add sautéed vegetables and ham to bean mixture. Cook over low heat 10 minutes, stirring occasionally.

Serve this delicious soup with a hunk of cornbread for the perfect ending to a chilly day.

Turnip Greens Stew

prep: 10 min. • cook: 35 min.

makes 6 to 8 servings

2	cups chopped cooked ham
1	Tbsp. vegetable oil
3	cups chicken broth
2	(16-oz.) packages frozen chopped turnip greens
1	(10-oz.) package frozen seasoning blend
1	tsp. sugar
1	tsp. seasoned pepper

start with...

❋ cooked ham

❋ frozen turnip greens

❋ frozen seasoning blend

1. Sauté ham in hot oil in a Dutch oven over medium-high heat 5 minutes or until lightly browned. Add broth and remaining ingredients; bring to a boil. Cover, reduce heat to low, and simmer, stirring occasionally, 25 minutes.

note: We tested with McKenzie's Seasoning Blend.

{ flavorful variation }

Collard Stew: Substitute 1 (16-oz.) package frozen chopped collard greens and 1 (16-oz.) can black-eyed peas, drained, for 2 packages turnip greens. Prepare recipe as directed, adding black-eyed peas during the last 10 minutes of cooking.

speed-scratch
SECRET

Frozen seasoning blend lets this soup come together in a snap, but you can also use one chopped fresh onion, one chopped celery rib, and one chopped green bell pepper.

An extra-large bouillon cube adds lots of flavor. If you don't have this size, you can use two regular cubes.

start with...

* frozen mixed vegetables

* canned tomato sauce

* canned tomatoes with seasoning

* chicken bouillon cube

speed-scratch
SECRET

Don't worry about thawing your vegetables; they'll warm quickly when added to the beef in the hot pan.

Beef Vegetable Soup

prep: 15 min. • cook: 1 hr., 5 min.

makes 12 servings

1½ lb. beef stew meat

1 Tbsp. olive oil

1 (32-oz.) bag frozen mixed vegetables (peas, carrots, green beans, and lima beans)

1 (15-oz.) can tomato sauce

1 (14.5-oz.) can diced Italian-style tomatoes

1 medium-size baking potato, peeled and diced

1 celery rib, chopped

1 medium onion, chopped

2 garlic cloves, minced

½ cup ketchup

1 extra-large chicken bouillon cube

½ tsp. pepper

1. Cook meat in hot oil over medium-high heat in a large Dutch oven 6 to 8 minutes or until browned.

2. Stir in frozen mixed vegetables, next 9 ingredients, and 1½ qt. water, stirring to loosen particles from bottom of Dutch oven. Bring mixture to a boil over medium-high heat; cover, reduce heat to low, and simmer, stirring occasionally, 55 to 60 minutes or until potatoes are tender.

note: We tested with Knorr Chicken Bouillon Cube.

Ham-and-Bean Soup With Fresh Spinach

prep: 15 min. • cook: 58 min.
makes 8 servings

1 (16-oz.) lean ham steak

2 Tbsp. olive oil

1 large onion, diced

1 bunch green onions, chopped

2 large carrots, diced

2 celery ribs, diced

1 Tbsp. jarred ham-flavored soup base

½ tsp. pepper

2 (15-oz.) cans navy beans, drained

2 (15-oz.) cans cannellini beans, drained

1 (15½-oz.) can black-eyed peas, drained

4 large Yukon gold potatoes, peeled and diced (about 2 lb.)

1 (5-oz.) package fresh baby spinach

1. Trim fat from ham steak; coarsely chop ham. Reserve bone.

2. Cook ham in hot oil in a Dutch oven over medium-high heat, stirring often, 6 to 8 minutes or until browned. Add diced onion and next 5 ingredients; sauté 5 minutes or until onion is tender.

3. Stir in reserved ham bone, navy beans, and next 3 ingredients; add water to cover. Bring to a boil; cover, reduce heat to low, and cook, stirring occasionally, 45 minutes. Remove and discard bone before serving. Stir in spinach just before serving.

start with...

* jarred soup base
* canned beans
* canned peas
* packaged pre-washed spinach

speed-scratch **SECRET**

This is a great way to use leftover holiday ham. You'll need about 2 cups to replace the ham steak. Don't forget to toss in the bone for added flavor.

prep:
10
min.

start with...

* frozen corn
* canned tomato puree
* canned tomatoes with green chiles

speed-scratch
SECRET

Use kitchen shears to quickly snip a stack of tortillas into strips.

Slow-cooker Chicken Tortilla Soup

prep: 10 min. • cook: 6 hr., 10 min.
makes 6 to 8 servings

2   (4-oz.) skinned and boned chicken breasts, cubed
2   cups frozen whole kernel corn, thawed
1   large onion, chopped
2   garlic cloves, pressed
2   (14-oz.) cans low-sodium fat-free chicken broth
1   (10¾-oz.) can tomato puree
1   (10-oz.) can diced tomatoes and green chiles
2   tsp. ground cumin
1   tsp. salt
1   tsp. chili powder
⅛   tsp. ground red pepper
⅛   tsp. black pepper
1   bay leaf
4   (5½-inch) corn tortillas

Garnishes: sour cream, fresh cilantro

1. Combine first 13 ingredients in a 4-qt. slow cooker. Cover and cook on HIGH 6 hours. Discard bay leaf.

2. Preheat oven to 375°.

3. Cut tortillas into ¼-inch-wide strips; place on a baking sheet.

4. Bake at 375° for 5 minutes. Stir and bake 5 more minutes or until crisp. Serve with soup. Garnish, if desired.

Mexican-Lime Chicken Soup

prep: 13 min. • cook: 20 min.

makes 8 servings

2   Tbsp. vegetable oil

1   large red bell pepper, chopped

1   large onion, chopped

1   tsp. jarred minced garlic

2   (14.5-oz.) cans Mexican-style stewed tomatoes, drained and chopped

2   limes

4   (14-oz.) cans chicken broth

3   cups chopped cooked chicken

¼   cup fresh cilantro

1   Tbsp. chopped pickled jalapeño pepper

¼   tsp. salt

¼   tsp. pepper

Toppings: shredded cheese, sour cream

Garnish: lime wedges

1. Heat oil in a Dutch oven over medium-high heat. Add bell pepper, onion, and garlic; sauté 3 minutes or until vegetables are tender. Stir in tomatoes and cook 2 minutes. Cut limes in half crosswise. Squeeze lime juice directly into vegetable mixture; add lime shells and chicken broth to soup. Bring to a boil; reduce heat, and simmer 10 minutes.

2. Remove and discard lime shells. Stir in chicken, cilantro, jalapeño, salt, and pepper. Cook 5 minutes or until thoroughly heated. Serve with toppings and garnish, if desired.

prep:
13
min.

start with...

✳ canned stewed tomatoes

✳ chopped cooked chicken

✳ pickled jalapeño pepper

speed-scratch
SECRET

Refrigerate leftovers in an airtight container up to 3 days, or freeze up to 1 month.

start with...

* bottled vinaigrette
* packaged sliced cheese

speed-scratch
SECRET

Make a double batch of the basil and mayonnaise mixture to use on sandwiches.

You won't miss the beef in these hearty burgers. These mushrooms have huge caps that have a meaty flavor and texture. Bottled vinaigrette makes a simple seasoning and basting mixture for the grilled veggies.

Grilled 'Bello Burgers

prep: 4 min. • cook: 10 min.

makes 4 servings

4	(4-inch) portobello mushrooms
4	(¼-inch) slices red onion
⅓	cup balsamic vinaigrette
¼	cup mayonnaise
2	Tbsp. chopped fresh basil
4	kaiser sandwich rolls
4	slices provolone cheese
4	green leaf lettuce leaves
4	(¼-inch) slices tomato

Pepper

1. Spray cold grill rack with nonstick cooking spray. Preheat grill to medium-high heat (350° to 400°). Place mushrooms and onion slices on grill rack; brush half of vinaigrette over mushrooms. Grill vegetables, covered, 5 minutes on each side or until tender, brushing mushrooms with remaining vinaigrette when turned.

2. Meanwhile, combine mayonnaise and basil; set aside.

3. To serve, spread mayonnaise mixture on bottom half of each roll. Top with mushrooms, onion slices, provolone cheese, lettuce leaves, and tomato slices. Sprinkle with pepper.

All-American Burgers

prep: 5 min. • cook: 18 min.

makes 4 servings

1   lb. lean ground beef
¼   cup spicy ketchup
1   Tbsp. Montreal steak seasoning
1   tsp. Worcestershire sauce
4   (1-oz.) Cheddar or American cheese slices (optional)
4   hamburger buns

Toppings: lettuce leaves, tomato slices, pickles, ketchup

1. Preheat grill to medium heat (300° to 350°). Gently combine first 4 ingredients in a large bowl. Shape mixture into 4 (4-inch) patties.

2. Grill, covered with grill lid, over medium heat (300° to 350°) 4 to 6 minutes on each side or until beef is no longer pink in center, topping each burger with 1 cheese slice during last minute of cooking, if desired. Grill buns, cut sides down, 30 seconds. Remove from grill, and place burgers on bottom halves of buns; top with remaining bun halves. Serve with desired toppings.

kitchen secret:
preparing the grill

We recommend cleaning your grill twice: once after preheating and once again when you've finished grilling. Use both a metal spatula and a wire brush to scrape the grates clean. Before grilling, coat the grill rack with cooking spray to keep the food from sticking.

prep:
5
min.

start with...

❉ spicy ketchup
❉ steak seasoning
❉ Worcestershire sauce
❉ packaged sliced cheese

speed-scratch
SECRET

Two quick tips for delicious burgers: Don't overwork the meat. And make a small indentation in the center of each hamburger patty to prevent a dome from forming.

start with...

✳ frozen meatballs

✳ mango chutney

✳ pickle sandwich
   relish

To make ahead, prepare meatballs as directed through Step 1. Store in an airtight container in refrigerator 2 to 3 days.

Meatball Sandwiches

prep: 10 min. • cook: 30 min.

makes 16 servings

32 bite-size frozen meatballs
1 (9-oz.) jar mango chutney
1 cup chicken broth
16 fresh dinner rolls
1 (16-oz.) jar sweet-hot pickle sandwich relish

1. Stir together first 3 ingredients in a medium saucepan. Bring to a boil over medium-high heat; reduce heat to low, and simmer, stirring occasionally, 25 to 30 minutes.

2. Cut rolls vertically through top, cutting to but not through bottom. Place 2 meatballs in each roll. Top with desired amount of relish.

note: We tested with Wickles Hoagie & Sub Sandwich Relish.

These sandwiches will be a winner with the family for their great flavor and with mom for the ease in preparation. They pair nicely with coleslaw either piled on top of the meat mixture or served as a side dish.

Super Simple Sloppy Joes

prep: 10 min. • cook: 20 min.

makes 8 servings

1½ lb. lean ground beef

1 (14½-oz.) can diced tomatoes, **undrained**

1¼ cups ketchup

½ cup bottled barbecue sauce

1 Tbsp. Worcestershire sauce

8 hamburger buns, toasted

1. Cook ground beef in a large skillet over medium-high heat, stirring until it crumbles and is no longer pink; drain well. Return cooked beef to skillet.

2. Stir in tomatoes and next 3 ingredients. Reduce heat to low, and simmer 15 minutes or until thickened. Serve mixture on toasted buns.

start with...

❋ canned diced tomatoes

❋ bottled barbecue sauce

❋ Worcestershire sauce

speed-scratch
SECRET

For a quick flavor kick, add some chopped pickled jalapeños (and some liquid from the jar) to get those taste buds jumping. Start with 1 tablespoon of each to suit your taste.

start with...

* **bottled salad dressing**
* **canned sauerkraut**
* **deli-sliced corned beef**
* **pimiento-stuffed olives**

speed-scratch
SECRET

Set up an assembly line of bread slices when coating the bread, layering ingredients, and stacking the triple-decker sandwich.

Grilled Reubens

prep: 12 min. • cook: 10 min.

makes 6 servings

1 (16-oz.) bottle Thousand Island dressing
18 rye bread slices
12 Swiss cheese slices
2 cups canned sauerkraut, drained
2 lb. corned beef, thinly sliced
Softened butter
Pimiento-stuffed olives (optional)
Wooden picks

1. Spread 1⅓ cups dressing evenly on 1 side of 12 bread slices. Layer 1 cheese slice, 2 heaping tablespoons sauerkraut, and about 4 slices corned beef over each prepared bread slice. Stack bread to make 6 (2-layer) sandwiches. Spread 1 side of each of the remaining 6 slices with remaining dressing, and place, dressing sides down, on sandwiches.

2. Spread butter over top of each sandwich. Place sandwiches, buttered sides down, on a moderately hot griddle or skillet; cook until bread is golden.

3. Spread butter on ungrilled sides of sandwiches; turn carefully, and cook until bread is golden. Skewer olives on wooden picks, if desired, and secure sandwiches with wooden picks.

Triple B Sandwiches

prep: 10 min. • **cook: 5 min.**

makes 6 servings

½ (4-oz.) package crumbled blue cheese

¼ cup butter, softened

½ (8-oz.) container chive-and-onion cream cheese

1 (12-oz.) package bacon, cooked and crumbled

12 slices pumpernickel or sourdough bread, toasted

12 oz. thinly sliced cooked roast beef

1 head green leaf lettuce, separated

2 tomatoes, thinly sliced

1 Tbsp. chopped fresh chives

1. Combine blue cheese and butter in a small bowl; set aside.

2. Place cream cheese in a small saucepan; cook over low heat, stirring constantly, until blended. Cool; stir in bacon.

3. Spread blue cheese mixture over half of bread slices; top evenly with roast beef, lettuce leaves, and tomato slices. Spread cream cheese mixture on remaining bread slices, and sprinkle with chives. Place, mixture sides down, on sandwiches.

kitchen secret:
chopping fresh chives

In order to chop chives safely, hold them in a bunch and place on a clean cutting board. Using a sharp knife, chop chives to desired size.

prep:
10
min.

start with...

✳ **packaged pre-crumbled blue cheese**

✳ **container of flavored cream cheese**

✳ **deli-sliced beef**

speed–scratch
SECRET

The chives for this recipe can be chopped ahead of time and stored in the refrigerator. Chop a batch of fresh chives at one time to have on hand for other dishes.

start with...

* bottled honey mustard
* container of flavored cream cheese
* deli-sliced ham
* packages of cheese slices

speed-scratch SECRET

Pulse the leftover bread in the food processor and store in the freezer in a zip-top plastic freezer bag for up to a month to keep on hand for quick access to fresh breadcrumbs.

Be sure to bring your appetite to feast on this large sandwich.

Giant Ham-and-Pepper Salad Sandwich

prep: 15 min.

makes 4 servings

1	(16-oz.) round Italian bread loaf
3	Tbsp. honey mustard
½	cup chive-and-onion cream cheese, **softened**
1	Tbsp. mayonnaise
1	lb. deli ham, **thinly sliced**
¼	cup pickled sliced banana peppers, drained
1	(6-oz.) package Swiss cheese slices
4	(1-oz.) American cheese slices

Tomato slices

Lettuce leaves

1. Cut off top one-third of bread loaf, and spread cut side of top with honey mustard; set aside.

2. Scoop out soft center of remaining bread, leaving a ¼-inch-thick shell. (Reserve soft center of loaf for other uses, if desired.)

3. Stir together cream cheese and mayonnaise; spread in bottom of bread shell. Layer with ham and next 5 ingredients; cover with bread top, honey mustard-side down. Cut into 4 wedges to serve.

A serrated knife or bread knife slices these sandwiches into clean pieces.

Warm Prosciutto-Stuffed Focaccia

prep: 10 min. • cook: 15 min.

makes 6 servings

1   (9-oz.) round loaf focaccia bread

3   oz. thinly sliced prosciutto

4   oz. thinly sliced Muenster cheese

1   (6-oz.) package fresh baby spinach

¼   cup bottled roasted red bell peppers, drained

2   Tbsp. light balsamic vinaigrette

1. Preheat oven to 350°. Cut bread in half horizontally, using a serrated knife. Top bottom bread half with prosciutto and next 3 ingredients. Drizzle with balsamic vinaigrette; cover with top bread half. Wrap in aluminum foil; place on a baking sheet.

2. Bake at 350° for 15 minutes or until warm. Cut focaccia into 6 wedges. Serve immediately.

start with...

❋ packaged pre-washed spinach

❋ bottled roasted red bell peppers

❋ bottled vinaigrette

speed-scratch SECRET

Look for focaccia bread in your supermarket's bakery. If you can't find it, a round Italian loaf or ciabatta bread can be used instead. Also, 6 ounces of ham may be substituted for prosciutto in this sandwich.

start with...

* canned pineapple
* packages sliced turkey and ham
* cranberry-orange relish

speed–scratch SECRET

Save the pineapple juice from canned pineapple to use to keep cut fruit such as apples and bananas from discoloring. Just toss the cut fruit in the juice, and then discard the juice.

Sweet raisin bread pairs deliciously with a sandwich filling of pineapple, ham, turkey, and cranberry relish.

Turkey and Ham Pine-Berry Sandwiches

prep: 8 min.

makes 6 servings

1   (3-oz.) package cream cheese, softened
⅓   cup drained crushed pineapple
12 raisin bread slices
1   (6-oz.) package low-fat smoked turkey breast slices
6   Tbsp. cranberry-orange relish, drained
1   (6-oz.) package low-fat cooked ham slices

1. Stir together cream cheese and pineapple. Spread 2 tsp. cream cheese mixture on each bread slice. Top 6 bread slices with turkey. Spread relish over turkey slices. Top with ham and remaining bread slices.

These roll-ups are a great way to sneak some greens into your day. For heartier appetites, these roll-ups will serve 6; or pair with a soup or salad to stretch them to 12 servings.

prep: **10** min.

Ham 'n' Turkey Roll-ups

prep: 10 min.
makes 6 to 12 servings

1 (8-oz.) container onion-and-chive cream cheese spread

½ cup chopped bottled roasted red bell peppers

6 (8-inch) flour tortillas

3 cups firmly packed baby spinach leaves

12 oz. sliced lean deli ham

12 oz. sliced deli turkey breast

1. Stir together cream cheese and peppers in a small bowl until smooth.

2. Spread about ¼ cup cream cheese mixture evenly over 6 tortillas. Place ½ cup spinach on each tortilla. Top evenly with ham and turkey slices. Roll up jelly-roll fashion, and cut in half. Secure each half with a wooden pick.

start with...

✳ container of flavored cream cheese

✳ bottled roasted red bell peppers

✳ packaged pre-washed spinach

✳ deli-sliced meats

speed-scratch
SECRET

Make these sandwiches ahead, chill overnight, and take them for a quick on-the-go lunch the next day.

prep:
11
min.

start with...

* preshredded cabbage

* package of grilled chicken strips

* mango chutney

speed-scratch
SECRET

Buzz the chutney on HIGH in the microwave 1 minute or just until warm.

Mango Chutney Chicken Pitas

prep: 11 min.

makes 4 servings

1   (10-oz.) package finely shredded cabbage
1   Granny Smith apple, diced
1   (6-oz.) container fat-free yogurt
1   tsp. lemon zest
½   tsp. dry mustard
2   (6-oz.) packages grilled chicken strips
1   cup warm mango chutney
4   pita rounds, halved crosswise

1. Combine first 5 ingredients. Layer chicken, mango chutney, and slaw mixture evenly inside pita halves.

note: We tested with Louis Rich Grilled Chicken Strips.

kitchen secret:
dicing an apple

Pierce the center of fruit with an apple corer, and rotate to remove core. Use a paring knife to slice in half vertically. Place apple halves, cut sides down, on a cutting board. Cut through skin to create apple wedges or thinner slices. Dice or chop wedges into smaller pieces with the paring knife.

Serve sandwiches with fresh fruit and oven-baked fries.

prep:
10
min.

Pesto Focaccia Sandwich

prep: 10 min. • cook: 10 min.

makes 6 servings

1   large deli-loaf focaccia or ciabatta bread
1   (3.5-oz.) jar prepared pesto sauce
½   lb. thinly sliced Black Forest ham
½   lb. thinly sliced roasted turkey breast
6   provolone cheese slices
½   small red onion, thinly sliced

1. Preheat oven to 450°.

2. Cut bread in half horizontally using a serrated knife. Spread pesto evenly over cut sides. Layer ham and next 3 ingredients evenly over bottom half. Top with remaining bread half. Wrap in aluminum foil.

3. Bake at 450° for 10 minutes. Cut into 6 wedges.

start with...

* jarred pesto sauce
* deli-sliced ham and turkey
* deli-sliced cheese

speed-scratch
SECRET

This sandwich can be assembled ahead. After you wrap the sandwich in foil, refrigerate until ready to bake.

kitchen secret:
using a serrated knife

Serrated knives, with their scalloped edges, are ideal for cutting through foods with a hard exterior and softer interior, such as crusty bread.

start with...

* package of cheese slices

* bottled pizza sauce

* jarred pesto sauce

Leftover bottled pizza sauce or pesto sauce will keep in the refrigerator several days. If you want to make this sandwich from ingredients on hand but don't have both sauces, one or the other sauce alone will make a yummy sandwich variation.

Grilled Pesto-Pepperoni Sandwiches

prep: 8 min. • cook: 8 min.

makes 4 servings

1	(6-oz.) package sliced mozzarella cheese, **cut into thirds**
8	Italian bread slices
¼	**cup** pizza sauce
¼	**cup** pesto sauce
20	pepperoni slices
2	Tbsp. butter, softened

1. Arrange 1 cheese slice on each of 4 slices of bread; spread evenly with pizza sauce. Top each with another cheese slice, and spread evenly with pesto sauce. Arrange pepperoni slices over pesto sauce; top with remaining cheese slices and remaining bread slices.

2. Spread half of butter on tops of sandwiches. Invert sandwiches onto a hot nonstick skillet or griddle; cook over medium heat until browned. Spread remaining butter on ungrilled sides of sandwiches; turn and cook until browned. Serve immediately.

BLT gone gourmet! This sandwich is fit for a queen with its unique blend of goat cheese, basil, garlic, and dried tomatoes.

BLTs With a Twist

prep: 13 min.

makes 4 servings

1   (4-oz.) package goat cheese, softened
1   Tbsp. mayonnaise
¼   cup chopped fresh basil
2   tsp. jarred minced garlic
¼   tsp. salt
¼   tsp. pepper
8   (1-oz.) sourdough bread slices, toasted
½   cup dried tomatoes in oil, drained and chopped
4   green leaf lettuce leaves
½   small red onion, thinly sliced
8   precooked bacon slices

1. Combine first 6 ingredients.

2. Spread cheese mixture evenly on 1 side of bread slices. Sprinkle tomato evenly over coated side of 4 bread slices. Top evenly with lettuce, onion, bacon, and remaining bread slices, coated sides down.

note: We tested with Oscar Mayer Ready to Serve Bacon.

start with...

* jarred minced garlic
* dried tomatoes in oil
* precooked bacon

speed-scratch
SECRET

Maximize the flavor of precooked bacon in this sandwich by heating the bacon in the microwave for 1 minute.

start with...

* jarred pesto sauce
* preshredded smoked chicken
* sliced fontina cheese

speed–scratch
SECRET

Pick up smoked chicken from the deli or your local barbecue joint, or use rotisserie chicken for this sandwich.

Smoked Chicken and Fontina Panini

prep: 7 min. • cook: 3 min.
makes 2 servings

1	(8-oz.) loaf ciabatta bread, cut in half horizontally
3	Tbsp. pesto sauce
2	plum tomatoes, sliced
1	cup shredded smoked chicken
2	slices fontina cheese

1. Preheat panini press according to manufacturer's instructions.

2. Spread bottom half of bread with pesto. Top with tomatoes, chicken, and cheese. Top with bread.

3. Place sandwich in panini press; cook 3 to 4 minutes or until cheese melts and bread is toasted. Cut into quarters and serve hot.

kitchen secret:
using a panini press

The popular Italian-style sandwiches known as panini are prepared in a special grill press that eliminates the need for turning. The top and bottom heating units cook sandwiches quickly and evenly, compressing and searing the bread to create distinctive ridges. Floating hinges on the press accommodate thick-sliced breads.

You can also use this egg salad to make finger sandwiches on thin white bread; or smear it on crostini, and top it with fresh herbs.

prep:
13
min.

Egg Salad Sandwiches

prep: 13 min.

makes 3 servings

6	large hard-cooked eggs
2	Tbsp. finely chopped celery
2	Tbsp. sweet pickle relish
3	Tbsp. mayonnaise
1	Tbsp. grated onion
¾	tsp. dried salad seasoning
½	tsp. Dijon mustard
¼	tsp. salt
¼	tsp. sugar
¼	tsp. freshly ground pepper
½	cup sliced pimiento-stuffed green olives
6	bread slices

1. Mash 3 eggs in a large bowl using a fork or pastry blender. Chop remaining 3 eggs. Add chopped eggs, celery, and next 8 ingredients to mashed eggs; stir until blended. Gently stir in olives. Cover and chill, if desired. Divide egg salad among 3 bread slices; top with remaining bread slices.

note: We tested with McCormick Salad Supreme Seasoning.

start with...

❋ package of hard-cooked eggs

❋ dried salad seasoning

❋ Dijon flavored mustard

❋ canned pimiento-stuffed olives

speed-scratch
SECRET

Look for packages of hard-cooked eggs in the deli or refrigerated section of your supermarket. They're prechilled and ready to use, and they're always cooked perfectly!

{ quick-fix soups & sandwiches }

Southern Classic

Nothing beats a delicious tomato sandwich. Thick slices of juicy red tomatoes pair with white bread, a hefty layer of mayo, salt, pepper, and a few sprigs of basil.

Dressed-up Tomato Soup

Pulse 1 (28-oz.) can Italian-seasoned diced tomatoes in a food processor 3 times. Stir together tomatoes; 1 (26-oz.) can tomato soup, undiluted; 1 (32-oz.) container chicken broth; and ½ tsp. pepper in a Dutch oven. Cook over medium heat, stirring occasionally, 10 minutes. Garnish with sour cream and basil.

toppings

Panini Bar

Let family members grill their own sandwiches. Some of our
favorite toppings include Gia Russa Bruschetta Toppings,
basil pesto, sun-dried tomato pesto, sun-dried tomatoes,
fresh basil, fresh mozzarella, roasted red and yellow bell peppers,
and artichoke hearts.

sides & salads in a flash

These fast and fresh side dishes and salads prove that veggies, pasta, and rice need not be overshadowed by the meat. Items such as frozen vegetables, prewashed lettuce, and bottled vinaigrettes help jump-start the preparation for scrumptious sides and salads. Many of these recipes can be totally or partially prepared a day or two ahead of time. Make every meal complete by serving one of these showstopping sides or salads.

205

One taste of these baked beans, and you'll think they've simmered all day long. But they're done in just 13 minutes. This recipe makes two servings, and it can easily be doubled or tripled to feed more people.

BBQ Beans

prep: 3 min. • cook: 13 min.

makes 2 servings

1   (15-oz.) can kidney or pinto beans, **drained**
3   **Tbsp.** brown sugar
1   **Tbsp.** dried onion flakes
¼   **cup** barbecue sauce

1. Combine all ingredients in a saucepan. Bring to a boil; cover, reduce heat to low, and simmer 5 minutes, stirring occasionally. Uncover and cook 5 more minutes.

kitchen secret:
maintaining a simmer

A constant simmer isn't always easy to regulate, especially on a gas stovetop. Even at the lowest setting, the heat can be too intense and cause the liquid to boil. Turning the flame too low can cause it to extinguish. To avoid this, put the pot to one side of the flame, or use a device called a flame tamer or heat diffuser to absorb some of the stove's heat.

start with...

❋ canned beans
❋ dried onion flakes
❋ bottled barbecue sauce

speed-scratch SECRET

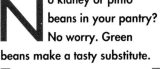

No kidney or pinto beans in your pantry? No worry. Green beans make a tasty substitute.

start with...

* frozen beans
* jarred minced garlic
* seasoned salt

speed-scratch
SECRET

Fry the bacon, and stir up the other seasonings while the butterbeans simmer; you'll be able to toss everything together in a jiffy.

Butterbeans are sweeter and more tender than lima beans. We preferred butterbeans in this recipe, but you could use either.

Bacon 'n' Herb Butterbeans

prep: 15 min. • cook: 34 min.
makes 4 servings

1   (16-oz.) package frozen butterbeans
4   bacon slices
4   green onions, sliced
1   tsp. jarred minced garlic
½   cup chopped fresh parsley
¾   tsp. seasoned salt

1. Cook butterbeans according to package directions; set aside.

2. Cook bacon in a large skillet until crisp; remove bacon, and drain on paper towels, reserving drippings in skillet. Crumble bacon, and set aside.

3. Sauté green onions and garlic in hot drippings 2 minutes or until tender. Stir in butterbeans, parsley, and seasoned salt; cook 1 minute or until thoroughly heated. Sprinkle with bacon.

"Succotash" is derived from an Indian word meaning "boiled corn kernels." This vegetable dish is made by cooking lima beans, corn, and sometimes bell peppers together. Bacon adds even more Southern flavor.

Creamy Succotash

prep: 15 min. • cook: 20 min.
makes 6 to 8 servings

1   (10-oz.) package frozen petite lima beans
1   (16-oz.) package frozen white whole shoepeg corn, **thawed**
2   Tbsp. butter
2   Tbsp. all-purpose flour
1   tsp. sugar
½   tsp. salt
½   tsp. seasoned pepper
1¼ cups milk
Garnish: precooked bacon, **crumbled**

1. Cook lima beans according to package directions; drain and set aside.

2. Pulse corn in a food processor 8 to 10 times or until coarsely chopped. Set aside.

3. Melt butter in large skillet over medium heat; add flour, stirring until smooth. Cook, stirring constantly, 1 minute; stir in sugar, salt, and seasoned pepper. Gradually add milk, stirring until smooth.

4. Stir in chopped corn, and cook, stirring often, 12 to 15 minutes or until corn is tender and mixture is thickened. Stir in lima beans. Garnish, if desired, and serve immediately.

start with...

✳ frozen beans
✳ frozen corn
✳ seasoned pepper
✳ precooked bacon

speed-scratch
SECRET

f you'd prefer simply to have creamed corn, just omit the lima beans.

start with...

✳ refrigerated green beans

✳ prechopped onion

speed-scratch
SECRET

Purchase one of the flavored tomato sauces and omit the vinegar for a change of pace.

Try this dish on the side for either a quick weeknight supper or casual get-together with friends.

Saucy Green Beans

prep: 10 min. • cook: 15 min.
makes 4 servings

1 (12-oz.) package refrigerated fresh green beans

¾ **cup** chopped onion

1 large garlic clove, minced

2 Tbsp. olive oil

1 (8-oz.) can tomato sauce

1 Tbsp. sugar

½ to ¾ tsp. salt

½ tsp. freshly ground pepper

1 Tbsp. red wine vinegar

1. Cook green beans in boiling water to cover 5 to 10 minutes or to desired degree of doneness; drain and set aside.

2. Meanwhile, sauté onion and garlic in hot oil in a large skillet over medium-high heat 5 minutes or until onion is tender.

3. Add tomato sauce and sugar; cook, stirring often, 5 minutes. Add green beans, salt, pepper, and vinegar; cook 5 minutes.

note: Substitute 1 lb. frozen whole green beans for fresh green beans, if desired. Cook according to package directions; drain well.

Here's a side dish worthy of the finest dinner menu. Fresh orange flavor and smoky chipotle pepper hit hot roasted broccoli and sizzle with goodness. Chicken, beef, or pork make fine partners.

start with...

* packaged broccoli florets

* canned chipotle peppers in adobo sauce

G rate the orange zest over wax paper for easy cleanup. Gently run the fruit up and down a microplane or the fine face of a box grater.

Roasted Broccoli With Orange-Chipotle Butter

prep: 2 min. • cook: 15 min.
makes 6 to 8 servings

2   (12-oz.) packages fresh broccoli florets
2   Tbsp. olive oil
¼   cup butter, softened
2   tsp. freshly grated orange zest
1   tsp. minced canned chipotle peppers in adobo sauce
½   tsp. salt

1. Preheat oven to 450°. Combine broccoli and oil in a large bowl; toss to coat. Place broccoli in a single layer on an ungreased jelly-roll pan. Roast at 450° for 15 to 17 minutes or until broccoli is crisp-tender.

2. While broccoli roasts, combine butter and next 3 ingredients in a large bowl. Add roasted broccoli to bowl, and toss to coat. Serve hot.

Serve this 10-minute vegetable with an entrée of your choosing for a quick and satisfying meal.

Orange-Curry Carrots

prep: 10 min. • cook: 5 min.
makes 4 servings

1   (1-lb.) package crinkle-cut carrots
⅓   cup orange marmalade
1   tsp. curry powder
½   tsp. salt
Freshly ground pepper (optional)

1. Place crinkle-cut carrots and 3 Tbsp. water in a microwave-safe bowl. Cover bowl tightly with plastic wrap; fold back a small edge to allow steam to escape. Microwave at HIGH 5 minutes or until tender. Drain.

2. Stir together orange marmalade, curry powder, and salt. Toss gently with hot carrots. Sprinkle with freshly ground pepper, if desired.

start with...

✳ **packaged cut carrots**
✳ **orange marmalade**

speed-scratch
SECRET

Orange marmalade makes a great glaze for vegetables such as carrots, which we enjoy a little on the sweet side.

start with...

✳ frozen corn

✳ precooked bacon

speed-scratch
SECRET

Here's our homestyle version of an Italian specialty—polenta. Be sure to add the cornmeal to the hot milk slowly, and stir constantly with a wire whisk. That way it won't have lumps.

Corn Pudding

prep: 10 min. • cook: 20 min.
makes 6 servings

2   cups milk
½   cup yellow cornmeal
1   (16-oz.) package frozen whole kernel corn, **thawed**
½   tsp. salt
2   Tbsp. whipping cream
Garnishes: chopped green onions, crumbled precooked bacon

1. Bring milk to a boil in a heavy saucepan; gradually add cornmeal, stirring until blended after each addition. Cook, stirring constantly, just until mixture begins to boil. Reduce heat, and cook, stirring constantly, until thickened.

2. Add corn, stirring until mixture is consistency of whipped potatoes. Stir in salt and whipping cream. Garnish with chopped green onions and crumbled bacon, if desired.

kitchen secret:
boiling liquids

Boiling cooks food at a relatively high temperature—212° is the boiling point for water at sea level. When liquids boil, bubbles break through and pop on the surface while the whole batch of liquid churns vigorously.

This spicy okra concoction will have you coming back for more.

Okra Creole

prep: 15 min. • cook: 25 min.
makes 4 servings

3   bacon slices

1   (16-oz.) package frozen sliced okra

1   (14.5-oz.) can diced tomatoes, undrained

1   cup frozen onion seasoning blend

1   cup frozen whole kernel corn

½   cup water

1 to 2 tsp. Creole seasoning

½   tsp. pepper

Hot cooked rice (optional)

Freshly ground pepper

1. Cook bacon in a Dutch oven until crisp; remove bacon, and drain on paper towels, reserving drippings in Dutch oven. Crumble bacon.

2. Cook okra and next 6 ingredients in hot drippings in Dutch oven over medium-high heat, stirring occasionally, 5 minutes. Reduce heat to low, cover, and simmer 15 minutes or until vegetables are tender. Top with crumbled bacon. Serve over rice, if desired. Sprinkle with freshly ground pepper.

start with...

✳ **frozen okra**

✳ **canned diced tomatoes**

✳ **frozen onion seasoning blend**

✳ **frozen corn**

✳ **Creole seasoning**

✳ **precooked rice**

speed-scratch
SECRET

Creole seasonings bring a great blend of herbs and spices, but be sure to read labels. Some brands are predominantly salt.

start with...

❋ jarred minced garlic

❋ frozen mashed
  potatoes

speed-scratch
SECRET

These garlicky mashed potatoes also would make a quick and easy topping for a shepherd's pie.

Buttermilk replaces some of the butter in these potatoes with outstanding results.

Buttermilk-Garlic Mashed Potatoes

prep: 10 min. • cook: 6 min.
makes 4 servings

2   Tbsp. butter
3   tsp. jarred minced garlic
1¼ cups buttermilk
⅔   cup milk
½   tsp. salt
½   tsp. pepper
1   (22-oz.) package frozen mashed potatoes

1. Melt butter in a Dutch oven over medium heat; add garlic, and sauté 1 minute. Add buttermilk and next 3 ingredients. Cook, stirring constantly, 5 minutes or until thoroughly heated. Stir in potatoes until smooth.

note: We tested with Ore-Ida Mashed Potatoes.

There's something about a really good vegetable casserole that's impossible to resist. This deep-dish favorite is a match for almost any entrée.

Easy Cheesy Potato Casserole

prep: 10 min. • cook: 49 min. • other: 5 min.

makes 6 servings

1   (20-oz.) package refrigerated hash browns

1   Tbsp. vegetable oil

1½ cups (6 oz.) shredded Mexican four-cheese blend

1   (10¾-oz.) can cream of mushroom soup

1   (8-oz.) container sour cream

⅓   cup chopped fresh chives

1   garlic clove, pressed

½   tsp. salt

½   tsp. freshly ground pepper

1. Preheat oven to 350°. Cook hash browns in oil in a large nonstick skillet over medium-high heat, stirring occasionally, 9 minutes or until golden brown.

2. Stir together hash browns, 1 cup shredded cheese, and next 6 ingredients. Spoon mixture into a lightly greased 8-inch square baking dish, and sprinkle with remaining ½ cup cheese.

3. Bake at 350° for 40 to 45 minutes or until edges are lightly browned. Let stand 5 minutes before serving.

start with...

❈ refrigerated hash browns

❈ preshredded cheese

❈ canned soup

speed-scratch
SECRET

Chop the chives ahead of time, and keep them in the refrigerator until ready to use.

start with...

* frozen butternut squash
* packaged chopped pecans

speed–scratch
SECRET

A s an option, you can use canned pumpkin puree or yams instead of the squash in this recipe.

Butternut squash is a yummy alternative to mashed potatoes.

Butternut Squash Casserole With Pecan Streusel

prep: 15 min. • cook: 40 min. • other: 5 min.
makes 8 to 10 servings

3   (12-oz.) packages frozen cooked butternut squash, **thawed**
1   cup firmly packed light brown sugar
½   cup half-and-half
¼   cup butter, melted
2   large eggs, lightly beaten
1   tsp. ground allspice
1   tsp. vanilla extract
¼   cup all-purpose flour
¼   cup firmly packed light brown sugar
3   Tbsp. cold butter, cut into pieces
½   **cup** chopped pecans

1. Preheat oven to 375°. Combine first 7 ingredients in a large bowl; stir well. Place in a lightly greased 11- x 7-inch baking dish.

2. Combine flour and ¼ cup brown sugar. Cut in 3 Tbsp. butter with a pastry blender until crumbly. Stir in nuts. Sprinkle over squash. Bake, uncovered, at 375° for 40 minutes or until edges are lightly browned. Let casserole stand 5 minutes before serving.

note: We tested with McKenzie Frozen Butternut Squash.

Spinach-Stuffed Peppers

prep: 2 min. • cook: 35 min.
makes 4 servings

1 (12-oz.) package frozen spinach soufflé, **thawed**
¼ cup Italian-seasoned breadcrumbs
2 small red bell peppers, cut in half lengthwise and seeded
Grated Parmesan cheese

1. Preheat oven to 350°. Combine spinach soufflé and bread-crumbs; spoon into pepper halves. Place in a shallow baking dish, and sprinkle with cheese. Cover and bake at 350° for 35 to 40 minutes. Sprinkle with additional cheese, if desired.

kitchen secret:
making breadcrumbs

Purchased breadcrumbs make cooking a snap, but homemade breadcrumbs are also easy to make and can be economical. You can make breadcrumbs from any type of bread and combine any varieties you have on hand. To make breadcrumbs, place the bread in a food processor, and pulse until the crumbs reach the desired consistency.

prep:
2
min.

start with...

✳ **frozen spinach soufflé**

✳ **seasoned breadcrumbs**

✳ **preshredded cheese**

speed-scratch
SECRET

Place the spinach soufflé in the refrigerator to thaw overnight so there's no need to thaw it in the micro-wave before using.

start with...

* canned sweet potatoes
* bottled orange juice
* packaged chopped pecans

speed-scratch
SECRET

Allspice tastes like a blend of cinnamon, nutmeg, and cloves although it's not.

Not just for the holidays, this super-easy recipe is great for weeknight dinners or to take to potluck suppers.

Bourbon Yams

prep: 10 min. • cook: 25 min.
makes 4 servings

1	(29-oz.) can cut sweet potatoes, drained and cut into ½-inch-thick slices
3	Tbsp. butter, melted
3	Tbsp. brown sugar
3	Tbsp. orange juice
3	Tbsp. bourbon
½	tsp. ground allspice
⅓	cup chopped pecans, toasted

1. Preheat oven to 350°. Place sliced potatoes in a lightly greased 8-inch square baking dish.

2. Combine butter and next 4 ingredients; pour over potato. Sprinkle with pecans. Bake at 350° for 25 minutes or until thoroughly heated.

note: If you're partial to fresh sweet potatoes, substitute 3 medium-size fresh (about 1½ pounds) for canned sweet potatoes. Cook in boiling water to cover 30 to 45 minutes or until tender. Let potatoes cool to touch; peel and slice.

Hot Tomato Grits

prep: 10 min. • cook: 25 min.

makes 6 servings

2   pieces of bacon, chopped

2   (14-oz.) cans chicken broth

½   tsp. salt

1   cup uncooked quick-cooking grits

2   large tomatoes, peeled and chopped

2   Tbsp. canned chopped green chiles

1   cup (4 oz.) shredded Cheddar cheese

Garnishes: chopped tomato, cooked and crumbled bacon,
  shredded Cheddar cheese

1. Cook bacon in a heavy saucepan until crisp, reserving bacon and drippings in pan. Gradually add broth and salt; bring to a boil.

2. Stir in grits, tomato, and chiles; return to a boil, stirring often. Reduce heat, and simmer, stirring often, 15 minutes.

3. Stir in 1 cup cheese. Garnish, if desired.

start with...

✳ **quick-cooking grits**

✳ **canned green chiles**

✳ **preshredded cheese**

speed-scratch
SECRET

Grits can be chilled and reheated. When reheating, whisk a tablespoon or two of warm water into grits over medium heat, adding more warm water as necessary.

prep:
5
min.

start with...

* microwaveable rice pilaf
* dried basil

speed-scratch
SECRET

Thanks to the availability these days of a variety of microwaveable products on the market, you can dish up a healthy serving of rice pilaf in less than 10 minutes.

With only four ingredients and just a 5-minute prep time, this makes the perfect weeknight side dish.

Basil Rice Pilaf

prep: 5 min. • cook: about 2½ min.
makes 4 to 6 servings

2   (8.8-oz.) pouches microwaveable rice pilaf
2   **Tbsp. chopped fresh basil or 2 tsp.** dried basil
2   **tsp. lemon juice**
2   **tsp. olive oil**

1. Microwave rice pilaf according to package directions; spoon rice into a serving bowl.

2. Stir in basil, lemon juice, and olive oil; serve rice pilaf immediately.

kitchen secret:
using fresh or dried herbs

The flavor of fresh herbs is generally better than that of dried; however, using fresh isn't always practical. Instead, substitute one part dried herbs to three parts fresh. This translates to 1 teaspoon dried for 1 tablespoon fresh. The exception is rosemary: Use equal amounts of fresh and dried.

This dish features chopped tomatoes and basil that freshen up jarred sauce in 15 minutes.

Tuscan Pasta With Tomato-Basil Cream

prep: 10 min. • cook: 5 min.

makes 4 to 6 servings

1   **(20-oz.)** package refrigerated four-cheese ravioli*
1   **(16-oz.)** jar sun-dried tomato Alfredo sauce
2   **Tbsp. white wine**
2   **medium-size fresh tomatoes, chopped****
½   **cup chopped fresh basil**
⅓   **cup** grated Parmesan cheese
Garnish: fresh basil strips

1. Prepare pasta according to package directions.

2. Meanwhile, pour Alfredo sauce into a medium saucepan. Pour wine into sauce jar; cover tightly, and shake well. Stir wine mixture into saucepan. Stir in chopped tomato and chopped basil, and cook over medium-low heat 5 minutes or until thoroughly heated. Toss with pasta, and top evenly with ⅓ cup grated Parmesan cheese. Garnish, if desired.

* 1 (13-oz.) package three-cheese tortellini may be substituted.

**1 (14.5-oz.) can petite diced tomatoes, fully drained, may be substituted.

note: We tested with Buitoni Four Cheese Ravioli and Classico Sun-dried Tomato Alfredo Pasta Sauce.

start with...

✳ packaged refrigerated ravioli

✳ bottled Alfredo sauce

✳ preshredded cheese

speed-scratch
SECRET

You can freeze refrigerated ravioli up to a month to have on hand for speedy suppers.

start with...

* canned sliced olives
* bottled balsamic vinaigrette
* packaged crumbled feta

speed-scratch
SECRET

If you don't have balsamic vinaigrette on hand, you can make a quick substitution with 4 Tbsp. olive oil; 2 Tbsp. balsamic vinegar; 1 small clove garlic, pressed; and ¼ tsp. dried oregano.

Toss in chopped cooked chicken or cooked shrimp for a quick one-dish meal.

Bow Tie Pasta Toss

prep: 3 min. • cook: 12 min. • other: 10 min.

makes 4 to 6 servings

8	oz. uncooked bow tie pasta
¾	tsp. salt, divided
1	cup grape tomatoes, cut in half
1	(2.25-oz.) can sliced ripe black olives, **drained**
1	Tbsp. finely chopped sweet onion
6	Tbsp. balsamic vinaigrette
½	(4-oz.) package crumbled feta cheese

Freshly ground pepper

1. Prepare pasta according to package directions, adding ½ tsp. salt to water; drain well.

2. Place pasta in a large bowl, and stir in tomatoes, olives, and onion.

3. Whisk together balsamic vinaigrette and remaining ¼ tsp. salt; add to pasta mixture, tossing to coat. Let mixture stand 10 minutes; stir in feta. Sprinkle with freshly ground pepper.

For extra flavor, you can add pre-cooked bacon to this scrumptious Southern favorite.

prep:
15
min.

Blue Cheese-and-Green Onion Potato Salad

prep: 15 min. • cook: 15 min.

makes 8 servings

3   lb. new potatoes, quartered
2   tsp. salt, divided
3   green onions, sliced
1   (8-oz.) container sour cream
½   **cup** refrigerated blue cheese dressing
½   tsp. freshly ground pepper
½   **cup** crumbled blue cheese
Garnishes: blue cheese, sliced green onions

1. Bring potatoes, 1 tsp. salt, and water to cover to a boil. Cook 10 to 15 minutes or just until tender; drain.

2. Stir together green onions, next 3 ingredients, and remaining 1 tsp. salt in a large bowl; add potatoes and crumbled blue cheese, stirring gently to coat. Serve immediately, or cover and chill until ready to serve. Garnish, if desired.

start with...

* bottled blue cheese dressing
* packaged crumbled blue cheese

speed-scratch
SECRET

This dish can be made ahead and chilled until ready to serve.

start with...

* packaged coleslaw mix
* precooked bacon
* bottled Ranch dressing
* packaged crumbled blue cheese

speed-scratch
SECRET

The gray-blue streaks in blue cheese are actually edible mold that helps produce the crumbly cheese with a tangy flavor. Blending the cheese with bottled Ranch dressing makes a tasty and quick homemade dressing.

After rinsing coleslaw mix with cold water, drain it very well to keep the shreds crisp. We like to drain it using a salad spinner.

Blue Cheese-Bacon Slaw

prep: 15 min.
makes 8 servings

2 (12-oz.) packages broccoli coleslaw mix
1 small onion, chopped
6 precooked bacon slices, crumbled
1 (16-oz.) bottle Ranch dressing
1 cup crumbled blue cheese

1. Rinse coleslaw mix with cold water; drain well. Combine coleslaw mix, onion, and bacon in a large bowl; toss mixture to combine.

2. Stir together Ranch dressing and blue cheese. Add to coleslaw mixture just before serving.

Cheese lovers can toss mozzarella cheese into this tasty and colorful salad.

prep:
15
min.

Italian Salad

prep: 15 min.

makes 8 servings

1   head iceberg lettuce, torn (about 1 lb.)

1   (9-oz.) package frozen artichoke hearts, **thawed**

1   (2.25-oz.) can sliced ripe black olives, **drained**

1   small red bell pepper, chopped

1¼ cups large-cut croutons

½   cup sliced peperoncini salad peppers

¼   cup chopped red onion

¾   **cup** refrigerated creamy Asiago-peppercorn **or**
     Parmesan-peppercorn dressing

1. Place lettuce in a 4-qt. bowl. Arrange artichoke hearts and next 5 ingredients over lettuce.

2. Top with dressing; gently toss to combine. Serve salad immediately.

note: We tested with Bolthous Farms Creamy Yogurt Dressing (Asiago blend) Caesar Parmigiano.

start with...

✳ frozen artichoke hearts

✳ canned sliced olives

✳ packaged croutons

✳ prechopped onion

✳ bottled salad dressing

speed-scratch
SECRET

No need to cook the frozen artichoke hearts—just thaw them and pat dry. Or you can substitute 1 (14-oz.) can artichoke hearts, drained.

start with...

* Creole seasoning
* bagged prewashed salad greens
* canned mandarin oranges
* bottled balsamic vinaigrette
* packaged crumbled blue cheese

T he pecans can be made ahead of time. Make an extra batch to have around for snacking or to save to use on a salad for another meal.

This salad is equally delicious served as a main dish topped with sliced beef, pork tenderloin, or grilled chicken slices.

Quick Baby Blue Salad

prep: 13 min. • cook: 10 min.
makes 7 servings

1½	cups pecan halves
1	Tbsp. sugar
2	tsp. Creole seasoning
2	(5-oz.) packages mixed salad greens
1	(11-oz.) can mandarin oranges, **drained**
1	pint strawberries, **quartered**
¾	cup balsamic vinaigrette
1	(4-oz.) package crumbled blue cheese

1. Preheat oven to 375°. Place pecans on a baking sheet. Heavily coat pecans with cooking spray. Combine sugar and Creole seasoning. Sprinkle over pecans; toss gently.

2. Bake at 375° for 10 minutes or until pecans are golden brown, stirring once. Cool thoroughly.

3. While pecans are baking, gently toss together greens, mandarin oranges, strawberries, balsamic vinaigrette, and crumbled blue cheese. Top with pecans.

note: We tested with Dole Spring Mix Salad Greens.

This colorful salad boasts a delicious combination of flavors—and it comes together in a snap.

Spinach-Grape Chopped Salad

prep: 10 min. • cook: 5 min.
makes 4 servings

2	Tbsp. pine nuts
1	(6-oz.) package fresh baby spinach
1	cup seedless red grapes, sliced
¼	cup crumbled reduced-fat feta cheese
¼	cup light raspberry-walnut vinaigrette

1. Heat pine nuts in a small skillet over medium-high heat, stirring constantly, 5 minutes or until toasted and fragrant.

2. Coarsely chop spinach. Toss together spinach, grapes, feta cheese, and vinaigrette in a serving bowl. Sprinkle with pine nuts, and serve immediately.

note: We tested with Newman's Own Light Raspberry & Walnut Dressing.

start with...

* packaged prewashed baby spinach

* packaged crumbled feta cheese

* bottled vinaigrette

speed-scratch
SECRET

I f you like your salad dressing a little creamier, add some nonfat or low-fat plain yogurt to thicken it.

start with...

✳ bottled vinaigrette

speed-scratch
SECRET

This dish can be made ahead of time. It pairs nicely with pasta, and is perfect to serve at a luncheon.

You can use all red tomatoes, such as a combination of cherry, plum, and beefsteak. But add other varieties and colors, when available, for a beautiful presentation.

Three-Tomato Salad

prep: 10 min. • other: 3 hr.
makes 8 servings

2   large yellow or red tomatoes, sliced
2   plum tomatoes, cut into wedges
1   pt. cherry tomatoes, cut in half
⅔   cup bottled vinaigrette
8   green leaf lettuce leaves
Salt and pepper to taste

1. Place tomatoes in a 2-qt. baking dish, and pour dressing over tomatoes. Cover and let stand 3 hours.

2. Place 1 lettuce leaf on each of 8 salad plates, and divide tomato mixture evenly among plates. Season with salt and pepper to taste.

note: We tested with Girard's Champagne Bottled Vinaigrette.

Avocado Fruit Salad

prep: 15 min. • other: 1 hr.

makes 6 cups

1   (24-oz.) jar refrigerated orange and grapefruit sections,
    rinsed, drained, and patted dry
1   (24-oz.) jar refrigerated tropical mixed fruit in light syrup,
    rinsed, drained, and patted dry
2   cups cubed fresh cantaloupe
1   medium-size ripe avocado, halved and cut into chunks
¼   cup chopped fresh mint
2   Tbsp. lime juice
Garnish: crushed pistachios

1. Toss together first 6 ingredients. Cover and chill 1 hour.
Garnish, if desired.

note: We tested with Del Monte SunFresh Citrus Salad and
Del Monte SunFresh Tropical Mixed Fruit in Light Syrup With
Passion Fruit Juice.

prep:
15
min.

start with...

❋ refrigerated orange
  and grapefruit
  sections

❋ refrigerated tropical
  mixed fruit

❋ cubed cantaloupe
  from the salad bar

❋ bottled lime juice

speed-scratch
SECRET

Y ou can prepare this
    salad a day ahead,
    but don't cut up the
avocado or add the garnish
until just before you serve it.

{quick-fix sides and salads}

It's in the Bag

Try prepackaged salads that usually can be found near the lettuce. They contain everything you need—even the dressing and the croutons.

Almost-Instant Potatoes

Whisk together 1 (1-oz.) package Ranch dressing mix, 1 cup sour cream, and 1¾ cups milk in a large glass bowl. Stir in 1 (22-oz.) package frozen mashed potatoes. Microwave at HIGH 12 minutes, stirring every 4 minutes. Stir in 6 cooked and crumbled bacon slices and ½ cup shredded Cheddar cheese. Garnish with sliced green onions.

PunchUp Potato Salad

Purchase a 32-oz. container of potato salad and add in ¼ cup chopped fresh cilantro, 3 chopped green onions, 1 tsp. lime zest, and 2 tsp. lime juice. Dip the rims of clear plastic cups in lime juice and then a mixture of pepper and barbecue seasoning. Serve the potato salad in the plastic cups, and garnish with lime wedges.

breads on the double

Baking up a batch of comforting, feel-good breads can be simple and quick with a few key ingredients. Baking mixes, refrigerated doughs, and bakery loaves you can jazz up make preparing fresh-from-the-oven favorites a snap. **Best of all, many of these breads and muffins are make-ahead and freezable, making it easy to prepare them according to your schedule.** Whether for breakfast, dinner, or just a midday snack, these simple recipes can be made in a hurry.

Due to the higher proportion of liquid to the dry ingredients, drop biscuits have a thinner batter than a soft dough such as rolled biscuits—which is why they're dropped instead of kneaded and rolled.

prep:
6
min.

Cheddar Drop Biscuits

prep: 6 min. • cook: 8 min.

makes 1 dozen

2   cups all-purpose baking mix

½   cup (2 oz.) shredded sharp Cheddar cheese

¾   cup milk

2   Tbsp. butter, melted

½   tsp. dried parsley, crushed

½   tsp. garlic powder

1. Preheat the oven to 450°. Combine baking mix and cheese; make a well in center of mixture. Add milk, stirring just until moistened.

2. Drop dough by rounded tablespoonfuls, 2 inches apart, onto a baking sheet coated with cooking spray. Bake at 450° for 8 minutes or until golden.

3. Combine butter, parsley, and garlic powder; brush over warm biscuits.

start with...

✳ baking mix

✳ preshredded cheese

✳ dried parsley

✳ garlic powder

speed-scratch
SECRET

Because they're dropped, these biscuits take a lot less time to prepare than the rolled variety.

start with...

* baking mix
* cornbread mix
* preshredded cheese
* fajita seasoning
* canned chipotle pepper in adobo sauce

The flavored butter will store in the refrigerator up to a week. Double the butter when making this recipe, and use the extra for jazzing up corn on the cob, baked potatoes, rice, or noodles.

Cheese Biscuits With Chipotle Butter

prep: 10 min. • cook: 10 min.

makes 2 dozen

1 (6.25-oz.) package all-purpose baking mix
1 (6-oz.) package cornbread mix
1 (8-oz.) container sour cream
1 cup (4 oz.) shredded Cheddar cheese
⅓ cup buttermilk
1 tsp. fajita seasoning (optional)
Chipotle Butter

1. Preheat oven to 400°. Stir together first 5 ingredients, and, if desired, fajita seasoning. Pat or roll dough out onto a lightly floured surface to ½-inch thickness. Cut dough with a 2-inch round cutter, and place rounds on a lightly greased baking sheet.

2. Bake at 400° for 10 to 12 minutes or until golden. Serve with Chipotle Butter.

note: We tested with Bisquick All-Purpose Baking Mix.

chipotle butter

prep: 5 min.

makes ½ cup

½ cup butter, softened
2 tsp. chopped fresh parsley
1 canned chipotle pepper in adobo sauce, diced
2 tsp. adobo sauce from can

1. Stir together all ingredients.

Spicy seasoned pepper blend makes these crisp breadsticks perfect for pairing with robust gumbo or stew.

Spicy Breadsticks

prep: 15 min. · cook: 10 min.

makes 4 servings

1 (11-oz.) can refrigerated soft breadsticks

1 large egg, lightly beaten

2 Tbsp. paprika

2 Tbsp. seasoned pepper blend

1. Preheat oven to 375°. Separate breadsticks; working with 2 at a time, roll each breadstick into a 12-inch rope. Brush ropes with egg. Twist ropes together, pinching ends to seal. Repeat with remaining breadsticks.

2. Combine paprika and pepper blend; spread mixture on a paper plate. Roll breadsticks in pepper mixture, pressing gently to coat. (Wash hands between rolling each breadstick, if necessary.)

3. Place breadsticks on a lightly greased baking sheet. Bake at 375° for 10 to 12 minutes.

note: We tested wtih McCormick Seasoned Pepper Blend.

start with...

❋ refrigerated breadsticks

❋ seasoned pepper blend

speed-scratch
SECRET

If you can't find seasoned pepper blend, combine equal portions of cracked black pepper, red bell pepper flakes, and salt.

Sour Cream Corn Sticks

prep: 5 min. • cook: 21 min.
makes 16 corn sticks

3   large eggs, lightly beaten
1   cup self-rising cornmeal mix
1   (8¾-oz.) can cream-style corn
1   (8-oz.) carton sour cream
¼   cup vegetable oil

1. Preheat oven to 400°. Heat lightly greased cast-iron corn stick pans in oven for 5 minutes.

2. Combine all ingredients, stirring just until cornmeal is moistened.

3. Remove cast-iron pans from oven, and spoon batter into hot pans.

4. Bake at 400° for 16 to 18 minutes or until golden.

kitchen secret:
measuring dry ingredients

Precise measurement is important in making quick breads. First, spoon the dry ingredients, such as cornmeal mix or flour, into a dry measuring cup. Then level off the excess with the flat edge of a knife.

Sweet nuggets of corn pack rich flavor in this buttery bread. One bite and this soufflélike dish could become a new favorite. Serve it warm from the oven; the dish firms up as it cools.

prep:
6
min.

Corn Spoon Bread

prep: 6 min. • cook: 35 min.
makes 12 servings

1 (8½-oz.) package corn muffin mix
1 (8¼-oz.) can cream-style corn
1 (8¾-oz.) can sweet whole kernel corn, **drained**
1 (8-oz.) container sour cream
½ cup butter, melted
2 large eggs

1. Preheat oven to 350°. Stir together all ingredients, and pour into a lightly greased 11- x 7-inch baking dish.

2. Bake at 350° for 35 minutes or until golden.

note: We tested with Jiffy Corn Muffin Mix.

start with...
※ packaged muffin mix
※ canned corn

speed-scratch
SECRET

Turn the oven on to preheat as soon as you start gathering ingredients together.

kitchen secret:
cracking an egg

Always crack an egg in a separate bowl before adding it to the mixture so that it's easier to find a stray piece of shell. Tap the egg on the side of the bowl until there's a small dent in the egg. Then pull the shell apart.

start with...

* ground cinnamon
* refrigerated crescent rolls

speed-scratch
SECRET

Working on a parchment paper–lined work surface makes cleanup a cinch, because there's no scrubbing butter and sugar off the counter. Plus dough doesn't stick to the pan.

These roll-ups are great for kids to make. They will have fun painting the melted butter onto the dough and rolling it up.

Cinnamon Toast Roll-ups

prep: 10 min. • cook: 10 min. • other: 1 min.
makes 8 rollups

¼ cup granulated sugar
¼ cup firmly packed light brown sugar
½ tsp. ground cinnamon
1 (8-oz.) can refrigerated original crescent rolls
2 Tbsp. butter, melted

1. Preheat oven to 375°. Stir together first 3 ingredients.

2. Unroll crescent roll dough onto a parchment paper-lined work surface. Separate dough into triangles. Brush with melted butter, and sprinkle evenly with sugar mixture.

3. Roll up each triangle, starting with shortest side; place on a parchment paper-lined baking sheet.

4. Bake at 375° for 10 to 12 minutes or until golden brown. Cool 1 minute on pan; remove to a wire rack to cool.

These quick and delicious breakfast treats are made using refrigerated cinnamon rolls.

Cinnamon-Apple Breakfast Buns

prep: 4 min.　cook: 20 min.

makes 8 rolls

1　(12.4-oz.) can refrigerated cinnamon rolls

1　(1.62-oz.) package instant cinnamon and spice oatmeal

¼　cup firmly packed brown sugar

¼　cup chopped pecans

¼　tsp. ground cinnamon

Dash of ground nutmeg

1　Tbsp. butter, melted

1　Granny Smith apple, peeled, cored, and cut into 8 rings

1. Preheat oven to 400°. Separate cinnamon rolls, and place in a lightly greased 8- or 9-inch round cakepan; set icing aside. Bake rolls according to package directions.

2. Meanwhile, stir together oatmeal and next 5 ingredients. Place 1 apple ring on each cinnamon roll; sprinkle mixture evenly over cinnamon rolls.

3. Bake at 400° for 20 to 22 minutes.

4. Remove top to icing. Microwave icing at LOW (10% power) for 20 seconds; drizzle evenly over rolls.

start with...

✳ refrigerated cinnamon rolls

✳ flavored oatmeal

✳ packaged chopped pecans

speed-scratch
SECRET

Pierce the center of the apple with an apple corer, and rotate to quickly remove the core.

start with...

✴ packaged chopped walnuts

✴ refrigerated biscuits

speed-scratch
SECRET

U se kitchen shears to quickly snip the biscuits in half.

This warm, gooey bread is swimming in sweet caramel. To enjoy it at its best, serve immediately.

Caramel-Nut Pull-Apart Bread

prep: 10 min. • cook: 30 min.
makes 12 servings

1   cup plus 2 Tbsp. firmly packed brown sugar
1   cup chopped walnuts
¾   cup butter, melted
3   (10-oz.) cans refrigerated cinnamon and sugar biscuits

1. Preheat oven to 350°. Combine brown sugar and walnuts in a small bowl. Stir in butter. Spoon half of sugar mixture in bottom of a lightly greased Bundt pan.

2. Cut each biscuit in half. Place half of biscuit halves alternately over sugar mixture. Spoon remaining sugar mixture evenly over biscuits in pan, and top with remaining biscuit halves.

3. Bake at 350° for 30 to 35 minutes or until browned. Invert bread onto a serving platter immediately, spooning any brown sugar sauce left in pan over bread.

note: We tested with Pillsbury Hungry Jack Refrigerated Cinnamon and Sugar Biscuits.

Broccoli Cornbread Muffins

prep: 10 min. • cook: 15 min. • other: 2 min.
makes 3 dozen mini muffins

1   (8½-oz.) package corn muffin mix
1   (10-oz.) package frozen chopped broccoli, **thawed and drained**
1   **cup (4 oz.)** shredded Cheddar cheese
1   **small onion, chopped**
2   **large eggs**
½   **cup butter, melted**

1. Preheat oven to 325°. Combine first 4 ingredients in a large bowl; make a well in center of mixture.

2. Stir together eggs and butter, blending well; add to broccoli mixture, stirring just until dry ingredients are moistened. Spoon into lightly greased mini muffin pans, filling three-fourths full.

3. Bake at 325° for 15 to 20 minutes or until golden. Let stand 2 to 3 minutes before removing from pans.

start with...

❋ packaged muffin mix

❋ frozen chopped broccoli

❋ preshredded cheese

speed-scratch SECRET

These muffins are a quick, flavorful treat for a breakfast or brunch menu. They also travel well, so you can take them anywhere from picnics to potlucks.

kitchen secret:
mixing dry and wet ingredients

Combine the dry ingredients in a large bowl, and make a well in the center for the wet ingredients. Pour the wet ingredients into the center of the well. Stir the batter just until moistened.

start with...

* packaged muffin mix
* dried blueberries
* container of fruit-flavored cream cheese

speed-scratch
SECRET

B e sure to mix the muffins just enough to blend the ingredients. And, when filling the cups, do not stir between spoonfuls. Overmixing will cause the loss of leavening and toughen the muffins.

With cream cheese inside of each muffin, these little gems offer a surprise with each bite.

Creamy Berry Muffins

prep: 10 min. • bake: 17 min. • other: 15 min.
makes 6 muffins

1 (7-oz.) package mixed berry muffin mix
1 (3.5-oz.) package dried blueberries
¼ cup fruit-flavored cream cheese

1. Prepare batter and muffin pans according to package directions for berry muffin mix, stirring dried blueberries into batter.

2. Spoon batter into prepared muffin pans, filling two-thirds full. Drop 2 tsp. cream cheese onto center of batter in each muffin cup. Bake and cool muffins according to package directions.

note: We tested with Martha White Wildberry Muffin Mix and Sunsweet Blueberries.

Easy, freezable, and delicious, these tasty treats make the ultimate quick breakfast or snack.

Cinnamon Streusel Muffins

prep: 15 min. • cook: 18 min. • other: 15 min.

makes 1 dozen

1   (15.2-oz.) package cinnamon streusel muffin mix
½   **cup** dried apple pieces, **roughly chopped**
½   **cup golden raisins**

1. Prepare cinnamon streusel muffin mix according to package directions, stirring dried apple pieces and golden raisins into batter. Place paper baking cups in muffin pans. Spoon batter into cups, filling two-thirds full. Bake and cool muffins according to package directions.

note: We tested with Betty Crocker Cinnamon Streusel Premium Muffin Mix.

start with...
❋ packaged muffin mix
❋ dried apple pieces

speed-scratch
SECRET

Try tossing the dried fruit in the muffin mix before adding liquid. This will prevent it from sinking to the bottom of the muffins.

kitchen secret:
chopping dried fruit

We prefer to chop dried fruit with either scissors or a knife coated with cooking spray. This keeps the fruit from sticking to the utensil, making the process go much quicker.

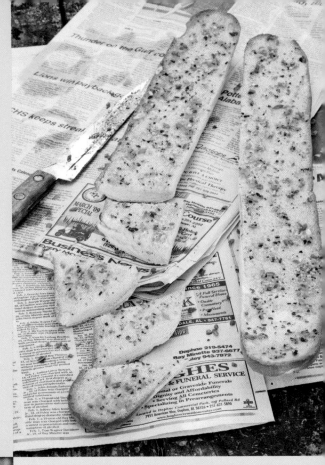

{ quick-fix breads }

Hot Off the Press Garlic Bread

Stir together 3 minced garlic cloves, 2 Tbsp. olive oil, 2 Tbsp. melted butter, and ½ tsp. crushed red pepper. Cut 1 (16-oz.) French bread loaf in half. Brush with garlic mixture; bake at 350° for 13 minutes or until golden. Sprinkle with chopped chives.

Herb Art

Stir together 1 egg white and 1 Tbsp. water. Brush mixture on top of bread; press fresh herbs onto dampened French baguette. Secure the herbs by gently brushing additional egg mixture on top. Bake at 350° for 5 minutes or until bread surface is dry.

Biscuit Beignets

Separate 1 (12-oz.) can refrigerated buttermilk biscuits into individual rounds, and cut into quarters. Pour oil to a depth of 2 inches into a Dutch oven, and heat over medium heat to 350°. Fry, in batches, 1 to 1½ minutes on each side or until golden. Drain on paper towels; dust with powdered sugar.

desserts in a dash

Luscious finales abound in many forms with these tantalizing sweets. Everything from cake mixes to instant puddings to pie fillings— even frozen biscuits—help these scrumptious sweets come together in a hurry. **Many of the recipes can be made ahead of time and stay fresh for several days...if they last that long.** Take your pick—you'll find a recipe to satisfy that craving for a little something sweet, even when you're short on time.

Banana Shortcakes With Candied Nuts

prep: 7 min. • cook: 23 min.

makes 6 servings

6	**large** frozen biscuits
2	**Tbsp. melted butter**
¼	**cup sugar, divided**
2	**small bananas**
1	**Tbsp.** lemon juice
¾	**cup whipping cream**
½	**cup chopped** Southern praline-style pecans

1. Brush frozen biscuit tops with melted butter; sprinkle each with ½ tsp. sugar. Bake biscuits according to package directions.

2. Meanwhile, slice bananas, and toss with lemon juice. Place half the banana slices in a small bowl, and mash until smooth; reserve remaining banana slices.

3. Beat whipping cream and remaining sugar in a medium bowl at high speed with an electric mixer until stiff peaks form. Fold in mashed banana and all but 6 reserved banana slices.

4. To serve, split warm biscuits, and spoon banana cream on bottom halves. Replace tops. Dollop with 1 Tbsp. banana cream mixture, sprinkle with chopped praline-style pecans, and top with one banana slice.

note: We used praline-style pecans as a topping for these shortcakes, but feel free to substitute other candied nuts or toffee bits as you desire.

prep:

7

min.

start with...

✳ frozen biscuits

✳ bottled lemon juice

✳ packaged praline-
   style pecans

speed-scratch
SECRET

Substitute thawed frozen whipped topping if you'd like. Instead of whipping and sweetening the cream, you'll need 1½ cups of the topping.

start with...

* package of gingersnaps
* crystallized ginger
* frozen cheesecake

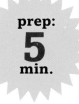

speed-scratch
SECRET

No need to worry about cutting neat slices on this cheesecake. Just spoon it into dessert bowls.

Ginger Streusel-Topped Cheesecake

prep: 5 min. • cook: 16 min.

makes 8 servings

1 **cup coarsely crushed** gingersnaps
½ **cup butter, softened**
½ **cup sugar**
½ **cup all-purpose flour**
1 **Tbsp. finely chopped** crystallized ginger
1 **(30-oz.) frozen** New York–style cheesecake

1. Preheat oven to 425°. Combine first 5 ingredients, mixing well with a spoon. Sprinkle streusel over top of frozen cheesecake. Bake at 425° for 16 to 19 minutes or until streusel is browned. Scoop warm cheesecake into serving bowls.

note: We tested with Nabisco Gingersnaps and Sara Lee Cheesecake.

{ flavorful variation }

Ginger Streusel-Topped Pumpkin Pie: Prepare topping as directed for cheesecake. Sprinkle topping over a small deli-baked pumpkin pie. Bake again at 425° for 18 to 20 minutes to brown the streusel. Let stand 15 minutes. Slice to serve. Makes 8 servings.

So-Easy Cherry-Fudge Cake

prep: 15 min. • cook: 27 min. • other: 1 hr., 10 min.

makes 12 to 15 servings

1   (18.25-oz.) package devil's food cake mix
1   (21-oz.) can cherry pie filling
2   large eggs
1   tsp. almond extract
1   cup sugar
⅓   cup milk
5   Tbsp. butter
1   cup semisweet chocolate morsels

1. Preheat oven to 350°. Beat first 4 ingredients at low speed with a heavy-duty electric stand mixer 20 seconds; increase speed to medium, and beat 1 minute. Pour batter into a greased and floured 13- x 9-inch pan.

2. Bake at 350° for 27 to 30 minutes or until a wooden pick inserted in center comes out clean. Cool cake in pan on a wire rack 10 minutes. Invert pan onto wire rack to remove cake.

3. Bring sugar, milk, and butter to a boil in a heavy 2-qt. saucepan over medium-high heat, stirring occasionally; boil 1 minute. Remove from heat; stir in chocolate morsels until melted and smooth. Quickly spread frosting over warm cake. Cool completely (about 1 hour).

note: We tested with Duncan Hines Moist Deluxe Devil's Food Cake Mix and Comstock Original Country Cherry Pie Filling or Topping.

prep:
15
min.

start with...

❋ cake mix

❋ cherry pie filling

speed-scratch
SECRET

nstead of removing the cake from the pan, you can frost it and store it in the pan, if you'd like.

start with...

* ✳ cake mix
* ✳ pudding mix
* ✳ packaged chopped pecans
* ✳ package of marshmallows

speed-scratch
SECRET

o toast the pecans, heat them in a small nonstick skillet over medium-low heat, stirring often, 3 to 5 minutes or until lightly toasted and fragrant.

Slow-cooker Rocky Road Chocolate Cake

prep: 15 min. • cook: 3 hr., 33 min. • other: 15 min.
makes 8 to 10 servings

1 (18.25-oz.) package German chocolate cake mix
1 (3.9-oz.) package chocolate instant pudding mix
3 large eggs, lightly beaten
1 cup sour cream
⅓ cup butter, melted
1 tsp. vanilla extract
3¼ cups milk, divided
1 (3.4-oz.) package chocolate cook-and-serve pudding mix
½ cup chopped pecans, toasted
1½ cups miniature marshmallows
1 cup semisweet chocolate morsels
Vanilla ice cream (optional)

1. Beat cake mix, next 5 ingredients, and 1¼ cups milk at medium speed with an electric mixer 2 minutes, stopping to scrape down sides as needed. Pour batter into a lightly greased 4-qt. slow cooker.

2. Cook remaining 2 cups milk in a heavy nonaluminum saucepan over medium heat, stirring often, 3 to 5 minutes or just until bubbles appear (do not boil); remove from heat.

3. Sprinkle cook-and-serve pudding mix over batter. Slowly pour hot milk over pudding. Cover and cook on LOW 3 hours and 30 minutes.

4. Turn off slow cooker. Sprinkle cake with pecans, marshmallows, and chocolate morsels. Let stand, partially covered, 15 minutes or until marshmallows are slightly melted. (The cake will look like it needs to cook just a little longer, but by the time the topping is set, it's ready to serve.) Spoon into dessert dishes, and serve with ice cream, if desired.

Mississippi Mud Cake

prep: 15 min. • cook: 41 min.
makes 15 servings

1   cup chopped pecans
2   (17.6-oz.) packages fudge brownie mix
1   (10.5-oz.) bag miniature marshmallows
Chocolate Frosting

1. Preheat oven to 350°. Place pecans in a single layer on a baking sheet. Bake at 350° for 8 to 10 minutes or until toasted.

2. Prepare brownie mix according to package directions; pour batter into a greased 15- x 10- x 1-inch jelly-roll pan. Bake at 350° for 25 minutes. Remove from oven, and top with marshmallows; bake 8 to 10 more minutes.

3. Drizzle warm cake with Chocolate Frosting, and sprinkle evenly with toasted pecans.

note: We tested with Duncan Hines Chocolate Lover's Double Fudge Brownie Mix.

chocolate frosting

prep: 10 min. • cook: 5 min.
makes about 2 cups

½   cup butter
⅓   cup unsweetened cocoa
⅓   cup milk
1   (16-oz.) package powdered sugar
1   tsp. vanilla extract

1. Stir together first 3 ingredients in a medium saucepan over medium heat until butter is melted. Cook, stirring constantly, 2 minutes or until slightly thickened; remove from heat. Beat in powdered sugar and 1 tsp. vanilla at medium-high speed with an electric mixer until smooth.

prep:
15
min.

start with...

✳ packaged chopped pecans

✳ brownie mix

✳ package of marshmallows

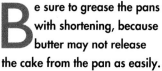

speed-scratch
SECRET

Be sure to grease the pans with shortening, because butter may not release the cake from the pan as easily.

start with...

❋ canned sweet
potatoes

❋ pastry shell

❋ whipped cream

speed-scratch
SECRET

Any time a recipe calls for an unbaked pastry shell, consider using refrigerated piecrust; you just unroll it into your pie plate and flute the edges. Looks like homemade.

It's easy to make your own pie for Thanksgiving. This one tastes so much fresher and looks prettier than store-bought pies.

Sweet Potato Pie

prep: 10 min. • cook: 45 min.
makes 6 to 8 servings

1   (14½-oz.) can mashed sweet potatoes
¾   cup milk
¾   cup firmly packed brown sugar
2   large eggs
1   Tbsp. butter, melted
½   tsp. salt
½   tsp. ground cinnamon
1   unbaked (9-inch) pastry shell
Sweetened whipped cream
Garnish: ground cinnamon

1. Preheat oven to 400°. Process first 7 ingredients in a blender until smooth, stopping once to scrape down sides. Pour into pastry shell.

2. Bake at 400° for 10 minutes. Reduce oven temperature to 350°, and bake 35 minutes or until a knife inserted in center comes out clean, shielding edges with aluminum foil after 20 minutes to prevent excessive browning. Let cool completely. Serve with whipped cream. Garnish, if desired.

Blackberry Cobbler

prep: 15 min. • cook: 45 min.

makes 6 to 8 servings

1⅓ cups sugar

½ cup all-purpose flour

½ cup butter, melted

2 tsp. vanilla extract

2 (14-oz.) bags frozen blackberries (do not thaw)

½ (15-oz.) package refrigerated piecrusts

1 Tbsp. sugar

Vanilla ice cream (optional)

1. Preheat oven to 425°. Stir together first 4 ingredients in a large bowl. Gently stir in blackberries until sugar mixture is crumbly. Spoon fruit mixture into a lightly greased 11- x 7-inch baking dish.

2. Cut piecrust into 1-inch-wide strips, and arrange strips diagonally over blackberry mixture. Sprinkle top with 1 Tbsp. sugar.

3. Bake at 425° for 45 minutes or until crust is golden brown and blackberry mixture is bubbly. Serve with ice cream, if desired.

prep:
15
min.

start with...

✸ **frozen blackberries**

✸ **refrigerated piecrust**

speed-scratch
SECRET

Make sugared sticks out of your remaining piecrust. Cut the piecrust into ½-inch-thick strips, and sprinkle evenly with 1 Tbsp. sugar. Bake at 425° for 6 to 8 minutes or until golden.

kitchen secret:
cutting piecrust

Use a pastry cutter to quickly cut the piecrust into strips.

prep:
5
min.

start with...

* box of buttery crackers

* chocolate kisses

* package of marshmallows

speed-scratch
SECRET

Line the baking sheet with aluminum foil for easy cleanup. Watch the little ones—the center of the marshmallow will still be warm after the 5-minute cooling time. The chocolate kisses will soften but not melt.

Yes, you can have the famous Girl Scout campfire treat without the bonfire. You'll love the slightly salty flavor the buttery crackers add compared to the traditional graham crackers.

S'more Puffs

prep: 5 min. • cook: 8 min. • other: 5 min.

makes 12 puffs

12 round buttery crackers

12 milk chocolate kisses

6 large marshmallows, **cut in half**

1. Preheat oven to 350°.

2. Place crackers on a baking sheet. Top each with 1 milk chocolate kiss and 1 marshmallow half, cut side down.

3. Bake at 350° for 8 minutes or just until marshmallows begin to melt. Let cool on a wire rack 5 minutes.

Don't think chocolate when you try these brownies. Instead, think pecans and sweet cream cheese topping.

Bayou Brownies

prep: 10 min. • cook: 40 min.
makes 8 servings

start with...

* packaged chopped pecans
* cake mix

1   cup chopped pecans
½   cup butter, melted
3   large eggs, divided
1   (18.25-oz.) package yellow cake mix
1   (8-oz.) package cream cheese, softened
1   (16-oz.) package powdered sugar

1. Preheat oven to 325°. Combine pecans, butter, 1 egg, and cake mix, stirring until well blended; press into bottom of a lightly greased 13- x 9-inch pan.

2. Beat remaining 2 eggs, cream cheese, and powdered sugar at medium speed with an electric mixer until smooth. Pour over cake mix layer.

3. Bake at 325° for 40 minutes or until set. Cool in pan on a wire rack. Cut into squares. Store in refrigerator.

speed-scratch
SECRET

f you forget to soften the cream cheese, buzz it in the microwave at HIGH for 15 seconds.

start with...

* refrigerated brownie batter
* package of assorted candies

speed-scratch
SECRET

These tasty little chocolate treats can be made ahead and frozen.

Nestle miniature chocolate candies into freshly baked brownie bites for impressive little chocolate treats.

Brownie Buttons

prep: 15 min. • **cook: 19 min.** • **other: 13 min.**
makes 20 brownies

1 (16.5-oz.) refrigerated roll triple chocolate chunk brownie batter
1 bag of assorted miniature peanut butter cup candies **and** chocolate-coated caramels

1. Preheat oven to 350°. Spray miniature (1¾-inch) muffin pans with cooking spray, or line pans with paper liners, and spray liners with cooking spray.

2. Spoon brownie batter evenly into each cup, filling almost full. Bake at 350° for 19 to 20 minutes. Cool in pans 3 to 4 minutes, and then gently press a miniature candy into each baked brownie until the top of candy is level with top of brownie. Cool 10 minutes in pans. Gently twist each brownie to remove from pan. Cool on a wire rack.

note: We tested with Pillsbury Refrigerated Roll Triple Chocolate Chunk Brownie Batter and Rolo candies.

Peanut Butter Brownie Bites

prep: 5 min. • cook: 50 min. • other: 1 hr.

makes 16 brownies

1   (19.27-oz.) package milk chocolate brownie mix
½   tsp. vanilla extract
1   (3-oz.) package cream cheese
⅓   cup creamy peanut butter
1   cup chocolate coated peanut butter candies

1. Preheat oven to 350°. Line bottom and sides of an 8-inch square pan with aluminum foil, allowing 2 to 3 inches to extend over the sides; lightly grease foil.

2. Prepare brownie batter according to package directions for fudgy brownies, stirring vanilla into batter. Pour batter into prepared pan.

3. Place cream cheese in a microwave-safe bowl. Microwave at HIGH 15 seconds. Add peanut butter, and stir until smooth and blended. Drop peanut butter mixture by 16 rounded teaspoonfuls onto batter. Sprinkle candies over batter.

4. Bake at 350° for 50 to 53 minutes or until a wooden pick inserted in center comes out with a few moist crumbs. Cool completely on a wire rack (about 1 hour). Lift brownies from pan, using foil sides as handles. Place on a cutting board, and cut into 16 squares.

note: We tested with M&M'S Peanut Butter Candies.

prep:
5
min.

start with...

✳ brownie mix

✳ jar of peanut butter

✳ package of chocolate coated peanut butter candies

speed-scratch
SECRET

Use a plastic knife to quickly and neatly cut the brownies into squares.

start with...

❋ jar of peanut butter

❋ baking mix

speed-scratch

SECRET

Leave the mixer in the cabinet—you can mix up this dough with a spoon.

The perfect pairing of two Southern favorites, these sweet treats are simply divine and super easy to make.

PB & Chocolate Pan Cookie

prep: 10 min. • cook: 20 min. • other: 5 min.

makes about 2 dozen

¾ cup chunky peanut butter

2 large eggs

1 tsp. vanilla extract

1 cup firmly packed light brown sugar

2 cups all-purpose baking mix

1 (12-oz.) package dark chocolate morsels, divided

1. Preheat oven to 325°. Stir together peanut butter, eggs, and vanilla in a large bowl.

2. Stir in brown sugar until combined. Add baking mix and ¾ cup dark chocolate morsels, stirring just until moistened. Spread mixture in a lightly greased 15- x 10-inch jelly-roll pan.

3. Bake at 325° for 20 minutes or until golden brown. Remove from oven, and sprinkle evenly with remaining 1¼ cups dark chocolate morsels; let stand 5 minutes or until chocolate melts. Spread melted chocolate evenly over top. Cut into triangles, bars, or squares.

prep:
15
min.

Peanut Blossom Cookies

prep: 15 min. • cook: 8 min. per batch
makes 4 dozen

1	**(14-oz.)** can sweetened condensed milk
¾	**cup** creamy peanut butter
1	**tsp. vanilla extract**
2	**cups** all-purpose baking mix
⅓	**cup sugar**
1	**(9-oz.)** package milk chocolate kisses**, unwrapped**

1. Preheat oven to 375°. Stir together condensed milk, peanut butter, and vanilla, stirring until smooth. Add baking mix, stirring well.

2. Shape dough into 1-inch balls; roll in sugar, and place on ungreased baking sheets. Make an indentation in center of each ball with thumb or spoon handle.

3. Bake at 375° for 8 to 10 minutes or until lightly browned. Remove cookies from oven, and press a chocolate kiss in center of each cookie. Remove to wire racks to cool completely.

start with...

✳ sweetened condensed milk

✳ jar of peanut butter

✳ baking mix

✳ package of milk chocolate kisses

speed-scratch
SECRET

Cookie scoops are handy for measuring dough. They scoop dough into a uniform size for drop cookies and help you nab the right amount of dough for rolling into balls as in this recipe.

speed-scratch
SECRET

Soaking the raisins in hot water plumps them up nicely.

Raisin-Oatmeal Cookies

prep: 10 min. • cook: 10 min. per batch • other: 6 min.

makes about 3 dozen

½   **cup** golden raisins

⅓   **cup hot water**

1   **(17.5-oz.)** package oatmeal cookie mix

½   **cup butter, softened**

1   **large egg**

1   **Tbsp. vanilla extract**

1. Preheat oven to 375°. Combine raisins and ⅓ cup hot water. Let stand 5 minutes; drain.

2. Stir together cookie mix and next 3 ingredients. Add raisins, and stir until blended. (Dough will be stiff.) Drop dough by tablespoonfuls 2 inches apart onto lightly greased baking sheets.

3. Bake, in batches, at 375° for 10 minutes or until golden brown. Cool on baking sheets on a wire rack 1 minute; remove from pans to wire racks.

note: We tested with Betty Crocker Oatmeal Cookie Mix.

kitchen secret:
dropping dough

Use one teaspoon (not a measuring spoon) to pick up the dough and another to push the dough onto the baking sheet.

Candy making has never been so easy! The slow cooker is the perfect tool to keep this candy mixture warm while you're spooning it out.

prep:
13
min.

Triple Chocolate-Nut Clusters

prep: 13 min. • cook: 2 hr. • other: 2 hr.

makes 6 dozen

1 (16-oz.) jar dry-roasted peanuts
1 (9.75-oz.) can salted whole cashews
2 cups pecan pieces
18 (2-oz.) chocolate bark coating squares, cut in half
1 (12-oz.) package semisweet chocolate morsels
4 (1-oz.) bittersweet chocolate baking squares, broken into pieces
1 Tbsp. shortening
1 tsp. vanilla extract

1. Combine first 7 ingredients in a 5-qt. slow cooker; cover and cook on LOW 2 hours or until chocolate is melted. Stir in chocolate and nuts; add vanilla, stirring well to coat.

2. Drop candy by heaping teaspoonfuls onto wax paper. Let stand at least 2 hours or until firm. Store in an airtight container.

start with...

✽ jarred dry-roasted peanuts

✽ canned cashews

✽ packaged pecan pieces

speed-scratch
SECRET

nstead of dropping the candy individually, spreading it thinly onto buttered jelly-roll pans is a quicker alternative. Just let it firm up, and then break into pieces like brittle.

{ quick-fix sweets }

No Fuss Chocolate Bar

Set up a chocolate station by picking your favorite candies at the grocery and arranging them decoratively. Break a candy bar into pieces, cut up a bakery brownie into bite-size pieces, and unwrap a few truffles.

Easy As ABC

Personalize bakery brownies by tinting ½ (16-oz.) container of ready-to-spread vanilla frosting with desired shade of food coloring gel. Spoon frosting mixture into a small zip-top plastic freezer bag. Snip a hole in 1 corner of the bag. Pipe the desired monogram on each brownie.

Quick and Tasty Banana Pudding

To make a single serving, cut half of 1 small banana into slices. Layer 1 (5-oz.) glass with 1 Tbsp. thawed nondairy whipped topping, one-fourth of banana slices, 1 Tbsp. prepared vanilla pudding, another fourth of banana slices, and 1 vanilla wafer. Repeat. Dollop with 1 Tbsp. thawed nondairy whipped topping. If you're serving a crowd, simply prepare the recipe as many times as needed.

metric equivalents

The recipes that appear in this cookbook use the standard U.S. method for measuring liquid and dry or solid ingredients (teaspoons, tablespoons, and cups). The information in the following charts is provided to help cooks outside the United States successfully use these recipes. All equivalents are approximate.

Metric Equivalents for Different Types of Ingredients

A standard cup measure of a dry or solid ingredient will vary in weight depending on the type of ingredient. A standard cup of liquid is the same volume for any type of liquid. Use the following chart when converting standard cup measures to grams (weight) or milliliters (volume).

Standard Cup	Fine Powder (ex. flour)	Grain (ex. rice)	Granular (ex. sugar)	Liquid Solids (ex. butter)	Liquid (ex. milk)
1	140 g	150 g	190 g	200 g	240 ml
¾	105 g	113 g	143 g	150 g	180 ml
⅔	93 g	100 g	125 g	133 g	160 ml
½	70 g	75 g	95 g	100 g	120 ml
⅓	47 g	50 g	63 g	67 g	80 ml
¼	35 g	38 g	48 g	50 g	60 ml
⅛	18 g	19 g	24 g	25 g	30 ml

Useful Equivalents for Liquid Ingredients by Volume

¼ tsp				=	1 ml
½ tsp				=	2 ml
1 tsp				=	5 ml
3 tsp	= 1 Tbsp		= ½ fl oz	=	15 ml
	2 Tbsp	= ⅛ cup	= 1 fl oz	=	30 ml
	4 Tbsp	= ¼ cup	= 2 fl oz	=	60 ml
	5⅓ Tbsp	= ⅓ cup	= 3 fl oz	=	80 ml
	8 Tbsp	= ½ cup	= 4 fl oz	=	120 ml
	10⅔ Tbsp	= ⅔ cup	= 5 fl oz	=	160 ml
	12 Tbsp	= ¾ cup	= 6 fl oz	=	180 ml
	16 Tbsp	= 1 cup	= 8 fl oz	=	240 ml
	1 pt	= 2 cups	= 16 fl oz	=	480 ml
	1 qt	= 4 cups	= 32 fl oz	=	960 ml
			33 fl oz	=	1000 ml

Useful Equivalents for Dry Ingredients by Weight

(To convert ounces to grams, multiply the number of ounces by 30.)

1 oz	=	1/16 lb	=	30 g
4 oz	=	¼ lb	=	120 g
8 oz	=	½ lb	=	240 g
12 oz	=	¾ lb	=	360 g
16 oz	=	1 lb	=	480 g

Useful Equivalents for Length

(To convert inches to centimeters, multiply the number of inches by 2.5.)

1 in			=	2.5 cm	
6 in	= ½ ft		=	15 cm	
12 in	= 1 ft		=	30 cm	
36 in	= 3 ft	= 1 yd	=	90 cm	
40 in			=	100 cm	= 1 m

Useful Equivalents for Cooking/Oven Temperatures

	Fahrenheit	Celsius	Gas Mark
Freeze water	32° F	0° C	
Room temperature	68° F	20° C	
Boil water	212° F	100° C	
Bake	325° F	160° C	3
	350° F	180° C	4
	375° F	190° C	5
	400° F	200° C	6
	425° F	220° C	7
	450° F	230° C	8
Broil			Grill

{index}